WE THE PEOPLE

# LANDMARKS OF
# PRINCE GEORGE'S
# ❧ COUNTY ❧

THE MARYLAND–NATIONAL CAPITAL PARK AND PLANNING COMMISSION

HISTORIC AMERICAN BUILDINGS SURVEY/
HISTORIC AMERICAN ENGINEERING RECORD, NATIONAL PARK SERVICE

ARCHITECTURAL PHOTOGRAPHS BY JACK E. BOUCHER

FOREWORD BY PARRIS N. GLENDENING, PRINCE GEORGE'S COUNTY EXECUTIVE

THE JOHNS HOPKINS UNIVERSITY PRESS, BALTIMORE AND LONDON

© 1993 Maryland–National Capital Park
and Planning Commission

The Johns Hopkins University Press
2715 North Charles Street
Baltimore, Maryland 21218-4319
The Johns Hopkins Press Ltd., London

LIBRARY OF CONGRESS
CATALOGING-IN-PUBLICATION DATA

Boucher, Jack E.

Landmarks of Prince George's County : architectural photographs / by Jack E. Boucher from the
Historic American Buildings Survey ; Maryland–
National Capital Park and Planning Commission ;
with a foreword by Parris N. Glendening.

    p.   cm.

Includes bibliographical references and index.

ISBN 0-8018-4628-5 (alk. paper)

    1. Historic sites — Maryland — Prince George's
County — Pictorial works. 2. Architecture —
Maryland — Prince George's County — Pictorial
works. 3. Prince George's County (Md.) — Pictorial works. 4. Prince George's County (Md.) —
History, Local. I. Maryland–National Capital Park
and Planning Commission. II. Title.

F187.P9B58  1993                         92-39873
917.52'51 — dc20                              CIP

Produced by Archetype Press, Inc., Washington, D.C.
Project Director: Diane Maddex
Art Director: Robert L. Wiser

Published in cooperation with the
Center for American Places, Harrisonburg, Virginia

This publication has been financed in part with federal funds
from the National Park Service, U.S. Department of the
Interior, made available through the Maryland Historical
Trust, an entity within the Department of Housing and
Community Development, State of Maryland. However, the
contents and opinions do not necessarily reflect the views or
policies of these agencies.

CONTRIBUTORS

Jack E. Boucher is photographer, Historic American Buildings Survey, National Park Service, U.S. Department of the
Interior.

Robert J. Kapsch is chief, Historic American Buildings
Survey / Historic American Engineering Record, National
Park Service, U.S. Department of the Interior.

Catherine C. Lavoie is historian, Historic American Buildings Survey, National Park Service, U.S. Department of the
Interior.

Susan G. Pearl is historian, Prince George's County,
Maryland–National Capital Park and Planning Commission.

Gail C. Rothrock is preservation coordinator, Prince George's
County, Maryland–National Capital Park and Planning
Commission.


Photographs: page 1, Greenbelt Center Elementary School.
page 2, His Lordship's Kindness. page 8, Bostwick. page 26,
His Lordship's Kindness. page 139, Mount Pleasant, Harmony Hall, Mount Lubentia, Coffren House, McEwen House.

# Contents

# Foreword

PARRIS N. GLENDENING, PRINCE GEORGE'S COUNTY EXECUTIVE

By celebrating some of Prince George's County's most important historic properties, this book anticipates the 1996 tricentennial of the county's founding. Prince George's County has seen great changes over the last three hundred years, from seventeenth-century settlements clustered along the major waterways to a sophisticated plantation society made prosperous by the production of tobacco. After the Civil War, small farms and local commerce became the dominant occupations, but by the mid-twentieth century Prince George's County had become part of the expanding metropolitan area of Washington, D.C.

Despite the extent of changes that have occurred, in many areas of the county Prince Georgians can walk along the creeks and rivers of the county's extensive park system and glimpse the rural character that the first settlers saw more than three hundred years ago.

Prince Georgians can be proud of the county's cultural legacy, including the landmarks pictured in this book as well as other historic sites, towns, and communities. The county's heritage is supported by many organizations that help promote the history and unique identity of each area of the county. Looking toward the tricentennial, these groups are supporting the effort to establish a heritage museum for all to enjoy.

*Landmarks of Prince George's County* documents the proud and still-visible history and architecture of Prince George's County. As county executive, I join the more than 730,000 Prince Georgians in inviting readers to help celebrate the county's tricentennial in 1996 — beginning with the fascinating history and images found within these pages.

*The porch of the P. A. Bowen House in Aquasco (see pages 102–03) has fine decorative detail. This elegant frame farmhouse was built for Philander A. Bowen in 1870.*

# LANDMARKS OF
# PRINCE GEORGE'S
# ～ COUNTY ～
# INTRODUCTION

# A Heritage to Preserve

GAIL C. ROTHROCK

The wealth of historic landmarks that remain in Prince George's County reflect the county's impressive agricultural heritage, its strong community institutions, and the growth of its early suburbs. That these landmarks stand today is a tribute to the foresight of property owners, preservationists, and government officials.

Prince George's rich architectural heritage was recognized as early as 1936, when the Historic American Buildings Survey photographed some ninety-seven early structures; today only sixty-five of those buildings are still standing. It was losses such as those thirty-two landmarks, and neglect of places such as Bowieville, Melwood Park, and the Ammendale Normal Institute, that galvanized county citizens into action. Now the county's landmarks are protected by a preservation ordinance and historic preservation master plan approved in 1981.

As the examples here show, historic buildings and communities provide the binding that connects the strands of our history. Houses, churches, schools, neighborhoods, farms, and historic landscapes all create the most tangible context for understanding an area's history and establish a link to the past. Landmarks provide a source of personal and communal memory and embody our architectural heritage.

Owners of historic properties in the county are partners in the stewardship of our cultural legacy, protecting and caring for their buildings so that they can be useful for years to come. The landmarks pictured here are both privately and publicly owned and represent a cross section of the county's history: plantation houses and dependencies, farmhouses, tobacco

*Weston's fanlighted doorway opens onto a view of the heart-shaped boxwood garden. The Weston property near Upper Marlboro (see page 84) has been home to nine generations of the Clagett family.*

barns, churches, meeting halls, a country store, a bridge, a train station.

Before the enactment of the county's preservation law providing for shared stewardship of our heritage, protection for historic properties usually came through acquisition by the county planning agency, the Maryland–National Capital Park and Planning Commission. The commission acquired historic properties as early as 1949, often because an important landmark was threatened with demolition or because the property was on land needed for another purpose. Today it owns two dozen historic properties.

PROTECTING COUNTY LANDMARKS

In 1969, three years after passage of the watershed National Historic Preservation Act, the commission undertook a survey of historic properties, identifying and mapping 186 in Prince George's County. The commission and the Maryland Historical Trust (the state historic preservation office) funded a project in 1973 to expand the 1969 inventory into a full-scale survey and to develop proposals for protection of the properties inventoried. This larger "windshield" survey, conducted between 1973 and 1975, identified more than 550 properties in Prince George's County. The 1975 survey was the basis for the listing of historic properties in the 1981 *Historic Sites and Districts Plan*.

When this plan and the preservation ordinance were approved in 1981, a nine-member Historic Preservation Commission was appointed to represent a wide variety of interests and disciplines. The preservation commission evaluates properties listed in an inventory of historic resources and can designate them as historic sites or historic districts. Designation decisions may be appealed to the Prince George's County Council. The commission also defines environmental settings; reviews and approves plans for exterior alteration, demolition, and new construction; and approves property tax credits for restoration and for new construction in historic districts.

Under companion legislation, the Historic Preservation Commission reviews land-use proposals affecting historic resources and makes recommendations to the Prince George's County Planning Board and County Council. Additional legislation passed in 1989 protects historic sites and their settings when land is being subdivided. Historic cemeteries are protected by a similar law. In 1992 the *Historic Sites and Districts Plan* was amended, adding thirty properties as historic sites and seventy-six as historic resources. Today more than 250 properties are designated as county historic sites, along with one historic district, the Broad Creek Historic District.

Prince George's County's preservation program has received the strong support of the county government, with staff assistance provided through two sections of the Maryland–National Capital Park and Planning Commission. The History Division in the commission's Parks and Recreation Department manages the restoration and interpretation of historic properties in the county park system; it also maintains research programs on archeology and black history. The Historic Preservation Section of the commission's Planning Department provides staff support to the Historic Preservation Commission, producing research on properties and historic communities, preparing materials for commissioners' review at public hearings, inspecting permit and tax credit applications, and continuing site and community survey work.

Federal Certified Local Government grants to support the Historic Preservation Commission have assisted in a survey and research program, covering more than 200 properties; research reports on towns, villages, historic roads, and landscapes; and preparation of more than twenty nominations to the National Register of Historic Places, including a nomination for a significant portion of a small city (Mount Rainier). Sixty individual county properties as well as four districts are listed in the National Register. In addition to the oldest sites, the county preservation program recognizes

*William Hilleary followed the stipulations of the Bladensburg commissioners and erected this substantial gambrel-roof house soon after he purchased his lot in 1743. It later was the home of Dr. Archibald Magruder.*

the importance of early to mid-twentieth-century architecture— from Sears, Roebuck mail-order houses to gas stations and the first suburban shopping centers.

## A PRESERVATION PARTNERSHIP

The Historic Preservation Commission works closely with two county-wide volunteer organizations, Prince George's Heritage, Inc., and the Prince George's County Historical and Cultural Trust. Prince George's Heritage took on the ownership and restoration of the Hilleary-Magruder House in Bladensburg; Heritage volunteers inspect protective easements on historic properties held by the Maryland Historical Trust and award seed grants for research and restoration projects. The Historical and Cultural Trust, the owner of Addison Chapel, has volunteers who operate the Newel Post, a salvage center where reusable architectural elements may be purchased.

Another long-standing preservation affiliate is the Prince George's County Historical Society, founded in 1952 and now headquartered at historic Marietta, owned by the Maryland–National Capital Park and Planning Commission. The society maintains a library of county history, publishes a monthly newsletter, and holds programs and special events for members, as well as guided tours and educational activities for the public at Marietta.

Reminders of the past are all around us. Throughout Prince George's County interest in preserving our long and varied legacy of historic sites and neighborhoods is growing. The challenges lying ahead for all of us include finding ways to provide support and incentives to owners of historic places, to preserve appropriate settings around historic sites even when zoning pressures tend to promote development, and to encourage preservation and conservation in older communities of the county. We have a unique heritage to preserve.

# Three Hundred Years of County History

SUSAN G. PEARL

For thousands of years before the first Europeans arrived, the land known today as Prince George's County was occupied by native Americans. Considerable evidence of their settlements can be found along both the Patuxent and the Potomac rivers; hundreds of prehistoric sites indicate the presence of many villages and temporary camps in the centuries before the arrival of European colonists. Contact between the native inhabitants and Europeans came in 1634, after the first Maryland colonists landed near the mouth of the Potomac River. Governor Leonard Calvert sailed up the Potomac to trade with members of the Piscataway tribe before establishing St. Mary's City, Maryland's first settlement.

The Maryland colony flourished at St. Mary's City and enjoyed peaceful relations with the neighboring tribes. The population increased, new counties were created, and within thirty years farms and plantations lined the Patuxent and the Potomac well into what is now Prince George's County. In the mid-seventeenth century all of this land was included in Calvert and Charles counties, established in 1654 and 1658, respectively; the land along the Patuxent was part of Calvert County, while that along the Potomac was part of Charles County.

By 1695 about seventeen hundred people lived in the area. The following year, on St. George's Day, April 23, 1696, a new county was established, named for Prince George of Denmark, the husband of Princess Anne of England. The new Prince George's County extended from the Charles County line on the south all the way to the Pennsylvania border, marking Maryland's western frontier. It remained the frontier county until 1748, when

*The south entrance facade of St. Paul's Church in Baden is highlighted by a rose window and an eighteenth-century sundial. St. Paul's (see pages 42–43) is the oldest church to survive in Prince George's County.*

the northern boundary became basically the line it is today.

Four years before Prince George's County was founded, the Church of England became the established church of the Maryland colony. When Prince George's County came into being in 1696, two parishes had already been created within its boundaries: St. Paul's in the area that had been part of Calvert County, and Piscataway (or King George's) in the area that was once part of Charles. At this time, there was already a church at Charles Town, the busy port on the Patuxent that was to be Prince George's first county seat. St. Paul's Parish had a rural chapel about twelve miles south of Charles Town, while in Piscataway Parish a church was built in 1696, at the site of present-day St. John's Church on Broad Creek.

THE EIGHTEENTH CENTURY

The land of Prince George's County was gradually settled during the 1700s. From all parts of the British Isles as well as the countries of Europe, men and women came—some free, others indentured servants. By the beginning of the eighteenth century, landowners had turned to slave labor for the operation of their tobacco plantations, and large numbers of Africans were brought to Maryland to work at the cultivation of that labor-intensive crop.

In 1706 the colonial General Assembly established five new port towns: Queen Anne, Nottingham and Mill Town on the Patuxent, Marlborough on the Western Branch of the Patuxent, and Aire at Broad Creek on the Potomac. A year later, Piscataway was established at the head of Piscataway Creek.

Marlborough developed more rapidly than the other port towns, and by 1718 it had become such an active center that its inhabitants petitioned to have the court proceedings moved there from Charles Town; the county court met for the first time in Upper Marlborough in 1721. From this time until early in the twentieth century, Upper Marlboro (as it is now written) was the commercial, political,

and social center of Prince George's County, and it has remained the county seat to this day. Charles Town, on the other hand, has ceased to exist: only the late eighteenth-century plantation house known as Mount Calvert stands on the site of this early port town.

In 1742 Bladensburg was established on the Eastern Branch of the Potomac. Commissioners were appointed to purchase sixty acres and lay out a town of sixty one-acre lots, most of which were sold right away. Each of the new owners was required to construct a 400-square-foot house, with a brick or stone chimney, within eighteen months of purchase. Bostwick, the Market Master's House, and the Hilleary-Magruder House are good examples of the earliest dwellings built in this important port town. Together with Upper Marlborough, Nottingham, Aire at Broad Creek, Queen Anne and Piscataway, Bladensburg became an official tobacco inspection station in 1747.

Although some industry was established, agriculture was the basis of the county's economy and directly or indirectly provided the livelihood for every resident. The heart of this agricultural economy was tobacco. It created the wealth that built fine plantation houses such as Compton Bassett near Upper Marlboro and His Lordship's Kindness near Rosaryville, educated the children of the leading families, and supported the work of the churches. It also provided the means to enjoy leisure time in activities such as fox hunting and horse racing and enabled planters to devote such care to their horses and their breeding that Prince George's County became the cradle of American thoroughbred racing. Tobacco created a sophisticated society that traded its staple for goods from all over the world.

Chief among the county's notable industries in the eighteenth century was the Snowden Iron Works, which provided wealth to the Snowden family and made possible the building of Montpelier, one of the county's grandest mansions. Water-powered mills also were built on the various tributaries of the Patuxent and Potomac rivers.

*A town house in Upper Marlboro that has evolved over the years, the Digges-Sasscer House has been the home of a series of attorneys who practiced law in the county seat. Its earliest section dates from the late 1700s.*

## THE REVOLUTIONARY PERIOD

Although the land of Prince George's County was spared the experience of actual battle, its residents were deeply involved in the great tide of events during the Revolution. Prince Georgians organized county committees and sent many of their sons to fight for the cause of independence. John Rogers of Upper Marlborough sat in the Continental Congress, which in July 1776 voted to make the colonies free and independent states. In September 1787 Daniel Carroll, also of Upper Marlborough, was one of the thirty-nine men who signed the newly framed Constitution of the United States. Four distinguished Prince Georgians attended the Ratification Convention in Annapolis in April 1788 and voted unanimously

in favor of approving the Constitution.

In 1790, when the Congress in Philadelphia decided to relocate the new federal capital, Prince George's County ceded most of the land necessary to establish the District of Columbia. The development of the capital was aided immeasurably by Benjamin Stoddert of Bostwick, who as George Washington's agent acquired much of the needed land. Stoddert later served as the first secretary of the navy.

After the Revolution two Prince Georgians assumed leadership roles in the newly independent churches of Maryland. Thomas John Claggett of Croom became the first Episcopal bishop consecrated in this country, and John Carroll of Upper Marlborough became the first Roman Catholic bishop in the United States. Beginning in 1783 the Catholic Church formulated its first constitution, meeting at White Marsh, one of the oldest Catholic establishments in Maryland.

## THE NINETEENTH CENTURY

Prince George's County was not spared military action during the War of 1812. In August 1814 the British sailed up the Patuxent to Benedict and marched through the county, camping at Nottingham and Upper Marlborough, and continuing past the brand-new Addison Chapel and north along the Eastern Branch of the Potomac (the Anacostia River). At Bladensburg they defeated poorly prepared American troops and continued into Washington to burn the capital city. On their way back through Upper Marlborough, they seized Dr. William Beanes and took him with them to Baltimore. Francis Scott Key was on a mission to plead for Dr. Beanes's release when he witnessed the bombardment of Fort McHenry and wrote the poem that became the national anthem, "The Star Spangled Banner."

Changes came to the county in the early years of the nineteenth century. Although tobacco remained predominant, farmers throughout Prince George's County began to experiment with new crops on land worn out by continuous cultivation of tobacco. The efforts of Charles B. Calvert of Riversdale brought about the establishment in 1856 of the nation's first agricultural research college, now the University of Maryland at College Park. Industries also were established here, employing machines, mass production, and hundreds of workers. In the early 1800s the first turnpike was constructed, linking Washington and Baltimore; about fourteen miles of convenient, nearly straight roadway ran through Prince George's County. In the 1820s the Snowden family established textile mills on the Patuxent River at a place soon to be known as Laurel. In 1835 the Baltimore and Ohio Railroad line was completed between Baltimore and Washington, bringing momentous change to the area, altering traditional methods of travel, trans-

forming small crossroads communities into population centers and, eventually, sites for suburban expansion. The railroad provided the right-of-way on which Samuel F. B. Morse strung the nation's first telegraph line in 1844.

Several Prince Georgians achieved distinction in nineteenth-century politics. Gabriel Duvall of Marietta sat for many years as an associate justice of the U.S. Supreme Court, and five other residents were elected governor of Maryland: Robert Bowie of Nottingham, Samuel Sprigg of Northampton, Joseph Kent of Rose Mount, Thomas G. Pratt of Upper Marlborough, and Oden Bowie of Fairview.

As the nineteenth century passed its midpoint, Prince George's County was prosperous, its society and economy solidly based on agricultural pursuits. But the old tobacco society was soon to end, as the nation plunged into the bitter Civil War. Prince George's County, like the state and the nation, was divided during that monumental struggle from 1861 to 1865. Although Maryland did not secede from the Union, there was great sympathy in the county for the southern cause. The county had a plantation economy and a population in 1860 that was more than half slave. The prominent families were slave holders and southern-oriented, and many of their sons went south to fight for the Confederacy. When the institution of slavery was abolished in the District of Columbia in 1862, many of the slaves in Prince George's County fled to freedom there. Emancipation took effect in Maryland in January 1865, bringing to an end the old plantation system. When the Civil War ended three months later, the old Prince George's society was gone, and the county began the difficult process of creating a second life.

## AFTER THE CIVIL WAR

The Civil War brought significant changes to Prince George's County; some were immediately noticeable, such as the freeing of the slaves. Small communities of blacks began to develop soon after the cessation of hostilities, such as Rossville near the Muirkirk Furnace and the black communities near Queen Anne and Upper Marlborough. Each of these communities was centered around a place of worship, usually Methodist, and in Rossville the residents established a benevolent society hall to provide aid to newly freed blacks. The newly emancipated citizens proceeded to build their homes, while supporting themselves working in the iron furnaces or railroad construction, but principally in farming. With the assistance of the Freedmen's Bureau, these communities soon had schoolhouses and teachers, beginning the significant movement toward black education.

Changes also occurred in the county's economy. Agriculture remained the predominant way of life. Tobacco continued to be the most important crop, and the large plantations by no means vanished. But in the last decades of the nineteenth century, small farms producing a variety of crops played a larger role in the county's economic life. Between the end of the Civil War and the turn of the century, the number of farms in Prince George's County doubled, while the average farm size decreased dramatically. Local commerce and the growth of towns such as Hyattsville played a part in the overall economic picture. Hyattsville had its beginnings in the mid-nineteenth century, when C. C. Hyatt established his store and post office at the intersection of the Baltimore and Ohio Railroad and the turnpike. In the 1870s Hyatt platted a residential subdivision; the community prospered and grew, becoming an attractive and desirable place to live. Within a decade, it was a thriving commercial center.

The county also was affected by the expanding federal government in the neighboring capital. As Washington grew from a small town to a major city, it began to spill over into the adjoining counties. A new phenomenon—the residential suburb—developed to accommodate the increasing number of federal employees and city workers. A new branch line of the Baltimore and Potomac Railroad had opened in 1872, joining with the main line to southern Maryland at the Bowie junction and creating a second rail link between Washington and Baltimore. In the 1880s and 1890s more and more residential communities were developed along both of the railroad lines, offering federal employees the opportunity to live away from the city in healthful surroundings easily accessible by rail. In towns such as Hyattsville, Takoma Park, Riverdale, Charlton Heights (now Berwyn Heights), and College Park, fine Victorian dwellings of the 1880s and 1890s still give evidence of this booming period of suburban expansion. As the nineteenth century drew to a close, the county's population was 30,000, thirty percent higher than it had been in 1860.

## THE TWENTIETH CENTURY

As the new century began, new types of transportation spurred additional residential development along the borders of the federal city. Brentwood and Mount Rainier, for example, grew up along the new streetcar line, which offered an easy commute between home and work. Several black communities (for example, North Brentwood and Fairmount Heights) were established, attracting members of an increasing group of black professionals from Washington. And although farming remained the way of life for many in the rural areas, the denser suburban population close to Washington continued to grow, spurred by the increasing use of the automobile; Cheverly, Greenbelt, District Heights, and Glenarden are examples of this trend. Prince George's had been a county of 30,000 in 1900; by 1930 its population had doubled, and by 1950 it had increased to almost 200,000. Population growth has continued, registering some 730,000 today. The 1990s promise a new and active image for Prince George's County: the development of professional-educational establishments, the revitalization of older communities, and the preservation of the county's proud heritage of historic resources and rural areas.

# Architecture: From Tidewater to Modern

CATHERINE C. LAVOIE

The architectural heritage of Prince George's County is rich and varied. Over the course of its three hundred-year history, the county has witnessed significant transformations in its architecture. Each era has been marked by leading styles and trends affected by regional and, later, national influences. The county's early architectural influences were decidedly Tidewater in nature, because southern Maryland was the origin of many of its first settlers. During the eighteenth century and well into the nineteenth century, the county economy was exclusively agricultural. Founded on a tobacco-growing, slave-based plantation system, this agricultural economy led to the adoption of the Georgian-style plantation house as a primary architectural form. Later changes away from symmetrical Georgian

designs to popular side-hall-and-double-parlor house plans reflect broader influences that paralleled national trends but still maintained a regional flavor. As the nineteenth century came to a close, the county witnessed a shift from rural farmsteads to residential communities, and Victorian styles, with their asymmetrical plans, came into popular use. This change marked the final assimilation with nationally recognized architectural styles in Prince George's County, as it did elsewhere. Suburbanization, facilitated by the rise of pattern-book and mail-order houses, continued as a trend throughout the twentieth century.

Prince George's County is probably best known architecturally for its eighteenth-century Georgian and Federal-period plantation houses. These grand masonry residences, dating roughly from the 1740s through the end of the eighteenth century, represent the peak

*Mount Pleasant, built about 1769 by John Waring, Sr., is a rare surviving early gambrel-roof house near Upper Marlboro. Its Tidewater style was popular during the period in which Prince George's County was first settled.*

of the county's architectural achievements and were among the first generation of substantial, permanent architecture. A whole century of architecture preceded them, however.

## THE TIDEWATER TRADITION

The county's first colonists, moving north along the Patuxent and Potomac rivers from the original settlements in southern Maryland, brought with them their southern Tidewater architectural traditions. Chief among them were houses with hall-and-parlor floor plans and 1½-story gabled or gambrel roofs. Most of these early houses were small, wood-frame structures too fragile to stand the test of time, so their existence is evidenced mainly through written documents. Much of the information about these buildings comes from the 1798 Federal Direct Tax, the first such survey of its kind. This document provides a wealth of information about individual buildings and plantations of the period. While a significant number of surveyed plantation houses measured well over 1000 square feet, the most frequent dimensions were much smaller, typically 28 by 20 feet. Only one in ten was of masonry construction; many had gambrel (referred to as hipped) roofs.

The Federal Direct Tax was not taken until 1798, but some of its notations (such as "old" or "very much out of repair") clearly indicate buildings that had been standing for several generations. These notations offer architectural information otherwise unavailable about these early county buildings: many were 1½ stories, with gambrel roofs and modest dimensions. These Tidewater characteristics prevailed even through the turn of the nineteenth century in carryover examples such as Belleview, near Friendly, and Snow Hill, near Laurel, evidenced by notations in the tax that such houses were "new" or "not yet finished." Thus, the Tidewater style imported by the early colonists dominated the architecture of Prince George's County for well over a century.

## EIGHTEENTH-CENTURY CHANGES

In addition to providing information on early buildings, the Federal Direct Tax of 1798 was also a barometer of change. The late eighteenth century appears to be the first significant period of architectural change, as the first generation of architecture was replaced or enlarged and new forms were introduced. Among the first indicators of change was an expanded floor plan that appeared in new houses. The early eighteenth-century form such as at Want Water—1½ stories, one room deep, with a boxed stairway and a gambrel roof—was replaced by an expanded plan, two rooms deep with an open stairway, in residences such as Wyoming. Georgian brick I-house forms of this period, such as at Melwood Park and Harmony Hall, which were one room deep with a center stairhall, by late century expanded to the two-room-deep, center-hall full Georgian form. This form was glorified in such outstanding Federal-style examples as Compton Bassett, Mount Lubentia, His Lordship's Kindness, Pleasant Prospect, and Montpelier. As the nineteenth century began, additions were often made to existing dwellings; the 1½-story, hall-and-parlor-plan Belleview, for example, had its roof raised and became two rooms deep, with an added stairhall. In many cases, connecting passages also were built to attach the formerly separate kitchen buildings to the main block, to put all rooms "under one roof." It was a period of tremendous architectural change and growth in the housing stock of Prince George's County.

## FEDERAL ELEGANCE

The expansion of house plans and the surge in building and remodeling that took place around the turn of the nineteenth century were brought about by a number of factors, for example, the prosperity of the tobacco trade and the diffusion of architectural styles and availability of building materials that came with the expansion of towns and trade routes estab-

*The unfinished interior walls of the kitchen wing at Wyoming (see pages 40—41), a plantation home near Piscataway, show early structural details such as timber bracing and brick nogging.*

lished for tobacco transport. In addition, a nationwide trend toward heightened social awareness created the need for specialized social versus family spaces. It was in this vein that the plantation houses of the county's elite planter class were built. These elegant brick houses, constructed roughly between 1780 and 1820, remained without equal in their display of architectural detail and their formal arrangement.

The new plantation dwellings clearly indicated the wealth of their inhabitants. The newly adopted two-story, four-room Georgian plan was far more imposing than the earlier forms. Rooms were more detailed, there were more of them, and an inordinate amount of space was devoted to the center stairhall reception area. These houses could boast two parlors, one for entertaining guests and the other for the private use of the family, with service areas kept far out of sight. The best parlor was designed to display elegant formality, while the family parlor was meant for familiar, multipurpose use. Mount Lubentia, Compton Bassett, His Lordship's Kindness, and Montpelier are among the county's finest examples of a new and formal plan: imposing size, grand entry halls and stairways, and large, finely detailed rooms.

## DEMOCRATIZATION OF ARCHITECTURE

By the 1830s another significant change was beginning to take place in architectural styles and the reorganization of household and domestic space. The Georgian and Federal-period mansion that had supplanted the Tidewater dwelling of the previous era was itself gradually supplanted by the side-hall-and-double-parlor form. This development away from the symmetrical Georgian style began to appear at the turn of the nineteenth century and established itself as a dominant form until the eve of the Civil War. This plan, paralleling national trends but maintaining a regional flavor, was used by planters and merchants alike, with decorative detail ranging from the most rustic to the near formal. It thus represents almost a democratization of the architecture of the county. The differences in the dwellings of this type were in size, materials (mostly frame, but a few of brick), and degree of detail. Woodstock, the Coffren House, Melford, and Pleasant Hills are good examples of this type.

## CIVIL WAR GENERATION

The Civil War brought to a close the plantation system on which the county's economy had been based. Whereas the period just before the war saw the peak of tobacco prosperity, the postwar era witnessed a substantial decrease in tobacco production and a temporary halt in population growth. As a result, little change occurred in the built environment during this time. The energies of the region were instead concentrated on diversification of agriculture and economic recovery. For the most part, no major architectural changes began to appear until nearly a generation after the Civil War; an exception is Bowling Heights, an outstanding example of High Victorian Gothic domestic architecture, built just a few years after the war. This house, however, was an exception; the county would never again see the grand plantation houses of the late eighteenth and early nineteenth centuries, built on the concentrated wealth of the slave-based plantation system.

Because the county had always been agriculturally based, little industrial or commercial development took place. What could not be produced on the plantation or farmstead was purchased at general merchandise stores located at crossroads throughout the county. The Coffren Store in Croom exemplifies the nineteenth-century store that was the essential feature of every rural crossroads community. The earliest center of industry and commerce was Laurel, where in the 1820s the Snowdens of Montpelier established textile mills near the Snowden Iron Works founded by the same family nearly a century earlier. Soon afterward, in the 1830s, the Baltimore and Ohio Railroad line was constructed through Laurel, by then an established town. Another iron works was built in the 1840s at Muirkirk, a short distance south of Laurel on the railroad line. At the time, these industries provided virtually the only nonagricultural jobs in the county, especially for blacks, a number of whom formed small communities in this area. In one of these areas, Abraham Hall was built as a benevolent society lodge; today it remains the focal point of the Rossville community.

## SUBURBIA ARRIVES

The next significant change in the architecture of the county did not come until the 1880s and 1890s, when the commuter railroad was introduced and suburban neighborhoods were formed. Residential communities were built along the Washington branches of both the B&O and Pennsylvania railroads in areas such as Hyattsville, Berwyn Heights, Riverdale, and College Park. Suburban development aimed at moderate-income families was in full swing nationwide during this period, creating both the need for an innovative house type, something between a town house and a country house, and a way to provide it cheaply and in volume. Thus, catalogues of house plans offered one means of designing and building suburban housing. This national trend is reflected in Prince George's County by houses designed by Robert W. Shoppell, one of the more successful "mail-order architects" of the era. Shoppell's designs reflect the popular architectural trends of Victorian America, with projecting bays and towers, wraparound porches, cross-gable roofs, polychromatic wall treatments, asymmetrical plans, and ornamental jigsawn trim. The O'Dea House in Berwyn Heights, built in the late 1880s, is one example of Shoppell's designs in Prince George's County. This design (no. 216) was described in the catalogue as having "fine, large rooms, a well lighted hall and stairway, good closet room, bath-room, back stairway, cellar, and a very attractive and comfortable veranda."

Suburban growth was further facilitated at the end of the nineteenth century by the establishment of trolley lines. In this way the county continued its move away from an agriculture-based economy, in which the majority of the population was tied to the land, to a population dependent on civil service and professional and business jobs in Washington, D.C. The national push toward suburbanization continued in the early twentieth century; the cost of suburban living decreased as more services and cheaper transportation became available. Closely associated with this trend was the rise of the small house, most notably the bungalow, seen in its many forms throughout the county today.

Together with suburban growth came the development of commercial centers. Hyattsville, for example, had by the 1880s become an attractive residential community with a thriving business center. A few of the turn-of-the-century commercial buildings remain, such as the Hyattsville Hardware Store. Many more, however, were replaced by the mid-twentieth century with low-scale commercial strip developments and more substantial buildings such as the Hyattsville Armory.

## THE MODERN PERIOD

One of the county's most significant examples of twentieth-century architecture is Greenbelt, a planned community developed in the late 1930s by the federal government. Its residential architecture is starkly modern and streamlined. The focal point of the community is the Green-belt Center School, built in the Art Deco style and ornamented by the sculptures of a Works Progress Administration (WPA) artist.

During the same period, a wealthier segment of society was constructing estate mansions in the Washington area. Although most of these grand homes were built on the north and west sides of the capital city, several fine examples in the county, such as the Newton White Mansion, survive.

## A CAPITAL INFLUENCE

Prince George's County, as one of the earliest and now one of the most developed counties in Maryland, is central to the timeline of the state's historic architecture. Over the past three centuries, the county's architecture has evolved from vernacular Tidewater traditions through academically inspired Georgian and Federal styles to nationally dispersed styles of the Victorian era and the early twentieth century. An important factor was the county's proximity to the nation's capital, whose founding coincides with the construction of many of the county's finest homes; the establishment of the capital undoubtedly provided architectural influences as well as confidence in the economic and cultural future of the county. Indeed, Washington was the impetus for the development of the western region of the county, where railroad and trolley lines linked Prince George's to the capital city. Here suburban development employed new architectural forms, such as pattern-book houses and simple bungalows, as well as a new outlook: politics and business rather than agriculture. Likewise, Greenbelt, intended as a national model, was located on the very doorstep of the federal government.

Prince George's County's architecture has developed and matured from vernacular traditions to nationally recognized styles reflecting a thriving metropolitan area. As each new tradition develops, it forms a vital link in the progression of the county's architectural heritage. This book proudly reveals some of the most outstanding examples of each of these periods.

# LANDMARKS OF PRINCE GEORGE'S

~ COUNTY ~

# IN PHOTOGRAPHS

# Documenting a County's Legacy

ROBERT J. KAPSCH

The Historic American Buildings Survey of the National Park Service, U.S. Department of the Interior, is the federal government's oldest preservation program. Established in 1933 to provide work for unemployed architects, HABS was continued well after other New Deal programs had been terminated. The measured drawings, large-format photographs, and written histories of historic structures prepared by the program have long been regarded as the national standard of excellence for architectural documentation. All materials are prepared to an archival standard of 500 years and are deposited in the Library of Congress's Prints and Photographs Division, where they are made available to the public. In fact, the HABS collection is one of the Library of Congress's most widely used special collections.

For the last decade, HABS has focused on documenting nationally significant historic buildings throughout the country. Recent examples of such projects include the White House, Monticello, the Battery in Charleston, South Carolina, the Lincoln and Jefferson memorials, and numerous others of our most important landmarks. Comprehensive records of these nationally significant structures are prepared so that interested scholars, researchers, and the general public will have a greater understanding and appreciation of America's built environment.

As important as it is to document nationally significant historic structures, HABS also is concerned with recording larger numbers of historic buildings. The methodologies used for nationally significant historic buildings — including a complete package of measured drawings, large-format photographs, and

*For approximately a century the Coffren Store (see pages 90–93) served as Croom's post office, a community institution in this rural area. The Coffren family built its house next door to this country store.*

histories—are not practical, cost-effective, or even desirable for the great numbers of historic buildings that are important to their communities and the nation. These structures may not be on the list of National Historic Landmarks—2,000 properties so far designated as nationally significant by the secretary of the interior—but they nevertheless are irreplaceable components of the nation's heritage.

## PILOT COUNTY-WIDE PROJECT

To this end HABS decided to undertake an innovative architectural documentation project that would rely on photodocumentation and focus on a single geographic entity, ideally a county. The plan was for HABS to work with an existing historic preservation agency to use its experience. Such an organization had to be professional and well versed in the history of its county. Also, because this approach was experimental in nature, we wanted a group that was within driving distance of the HABS office in Washington, D.C.; close proximity would enhance the interaction between the two staffs. HABS assessed nearby localities, based on the depth and breadth of professional staff involved in historic preservation activities, the reputation of the preservation organization, leadership, and the overall quality of architecture in the county.

Based on that assessment, we decided to select the Prince George's County Historic Preservation Commission. Prince George's County, Maryland, located immediately southeast of Washington, D.C., met our criteria for accessibility. We also knew that Prince George's County had a rich collection of historic structures—probably the richest in the greater Washington, D.C., metropolitan area. Furthermore, the Historic Preservation Commission staff was widely regarded as being extremely competent and knowledgeable about the county's historic resources. Finally, we knew well the work of the county's historic preservation coordinator, Gail C. Rothrock,

particularly her work in upper Montgomery County, Maryland. For these reasons we decided to make Prince George's County the subject of our first county photodocumentation project.

We approached Prince George's County with our proposal to undertake a pilot project in close cooperation with the Historic Preservation Commission. HABS was warmly welcomed by the staff as well as the Prince George's Planning Board and Prince George's County Executive Parris Glendening, who gave his support over the life of the recording project.

## SELECTION OF SITES

An agreement with the Maryland–National Capital Park and Planning Commission was signed in July 1988, and the HABS pilot project began in February 1989. Historic structures to be documented were selected to represent a variety of periods, styles, and regions of the county. They included thirty-seven of the county's sixty properties that are listed in the National Register of Historic Places, as well as others among the more than 250 properties designated as county historic sites (see pages 135–38). The selection process settled on representative examples of building periods and types: the early Tidewater, Georgian, Federal, Greek Revival, and Queen Anne styles in houses and churches, a store from the 1840s with its interior features intact, a Victorian train station, and an Art Deco school, as well as an early nineteenth-century tobacco barn and a rich collection of outbuildings.

## DOCUMENTATION BEGINS

Over the next three years HABS documented sixty-two historic structures in the county with 900 large-format (5 by 7 inches), archivally processed photographs taken by HABS photographer Jack E. Boucher, a thirty-year staff member whose work has established exceptional standards for architectural photography nationwide. Historian Catherine C. Lavoie served as the HABS project leader and accompanied Mr. Boucher in the field, interviewing building owners and, with the help of historian Susan G. Pearl from the Prince George's County Planning Department, collecting information to be entered into the HABS collection in the Library of Congress.

## SHARING THE RESULTS

By May 1989 the first photographs were ready to be exhibited at the county's annual celebration of National Historic Preservation Week. During the course of the project, the photographs were presented in a number of other exhibits around the county, including at Montpelier in Laurel, the Publick Playhouse in Cheverly, and the Harmony Hall Regional Center in Broad Creek. The work culminated in a major exhibition at the historic Arts Club in Washington in February 1991.

Reviewing the project on the steps of Montpelier one fine autumn day, Gail Rothrock and I agreed that the beauty, variety, and richness of the architectural heritage of Prince George's County should be brought to a much larger audience than could attend the photographic exhibits. We then decided to pursue publication of a book that would demonstrate the rich legacy that the HABS project had only sampled. As a result, Archetype Press in Washington was enlisted to explore production of a publication to achieve this goal. It was Diane Maddex, president of Archetype Press and a long-standing supporter of HABS and publisher of many books using HABS documentation, who linked us up with George F. Thompson, president of the Center for American Places and a publishing consultant to the renowned Johns Hopkins University Press.

*Landmarks of Prince George's County* represents a unique experiment between a federal agency and a local agency to document in an innovative process the architectural heritage of one of America's most historic counties. The staff of the Historic American Buildings Survey worked closely with the staff of the Prince George's County historic preservation office to complete this pilot project, although many other people contributed to the success of the effort.

## A RICH LEGACY

As you review the photographs and captions that follow, you will see for yourself the rich array of buildings and other historic structures that can be found in Prince George's County. The entries are arranged in chronological order to capture the evolution of the county's architectural and historical development. The book, however, shows only a portion of the county's legacy. From some 900 photographs taken, 125 images were chosen to highlight the county's landmarks.

The complete record—the photographs and histories—will become part of the HABS collection in the Library of Congress and will be made available for use by the public, to research historic structures and to obtain copies of the photographs. A photodocumentation project of this magnitude, with limits on time and funding, could not have included all of the historic buildings in Prince George's County. Our hope is that the county's entire group of designated historic sites may also be included in the HABS collection in the future.

The quality of the images shown here—so important for any architectural photography book—stems from two primary sources. First, the experience of HABS photographer Jack Boucher, working in large format, ensured the best possible images. Second, the book has been written, designed, and published with great care by all the parties involved.

For HABS, this project has been an immense and rewarding success—one that we hope will inspire similar efforts in other areas of the country. Its success is a product of the strong and continuing support of the many preservation-minded people who live and work in Prince George's County.

## DARNALL'S CHANCE

*Darnall's Chance in Upper Marlboro, built about 1700, was probably the birthplace of John Carroll, the founder of Georgetown University and first Roman Catholic bishop in America, and his brother, Daniel Carroll II, a member of the Continental and U.S. congresses. Extensively remodeled in 1858, this elaborate mansion was purchased in 1974 by the Maryland–National Capital Park and Planning Commission to build a parking garage on the site. Because of its significance it was, instead, rebuilt to reflect its original configuration. ✦ An eighteenth-century burial vault, recently uncovered by archeologists, contained the remains of several past owners, probably the family of Dr. Adam Thompson, as documented in a 1788 deed that reserved the family's rights to visit the vault after the sale of the property. Artifacts and household items discarded there reveal much about the lifestyles of the early residents of Darnall's Chance.*

*The historically documented features of Want Water on Broad Creek indicate that this was once the home of a family of distinction. All that remains today are two brick end walls with chimneys, hand-hewn sills, the summer beam, and stone foundations. ⊛ Want Water was built for Colonel Thomas Addison, the first county surveyor, soon after 1706–07. The property remained in the Addison family until 1736. In 1761 it was purchased by Enoch Magruder, who also was a wealthy county landholder. The house evidently was occupied by his daughter, Sarah, and her husband, Colonel William Lyles, and it remained in their family until 1845. ⊛ Want Water's ruins present significant information about the construction techniques and architecture of the period. It had a gambrel roof and interior details such as paneled and plastered walls and large round-arch fireplaces. Although representative of Tidewater-style dwellings of the time, Want Water was unusual in its substantial construction, fine details, and its center-hall plan. ⊛ Later occupied by tenants and eventually abandoned, Want Water was already in a deteriorated state when it was first photographed by the Historic American Buildings Survey in 1936.*

## BELAIR MANSION

Horse racing was a popular pastime in Prince George's County in the 1740s, when Belair Mansion in Bowie was built for Provincial Governor Samuel Ogle. Together with its later stables (see pages 124–25), Belair symbolizes more than 250 years of thoroughbred horse racing. ⊛ An outstanding example of Georgian architecture, the main block is 2½ stories high, built of brick, with a projecting central pedimented pavilion and low-pitched hip-on-hip roof. Flanking this are lower two-story wings, also of brick, which were built early in the twentieth century. ⊛ Belair passed to Samuel Ogle's son

Benjamin, who was governor of Maryland from 1798 to 1801, and it remained the home of Ogle descendants until after the Civil War. In 1898 Belair was purchased by James T. Woodward; he and his nephew, William Woodward, added the flanking hyphens and wings, completing the house's evolution to a five-part mansion. They also continued the Ogles' thoroughbred tradition, bringing it into the modern era. In the 1950s the Belair estate was purchased by the Levitt Corporation, which developed the grounds into residential lots. Today it is owned and administered by the city of Bowie as a museum.

## HARMONY HALL

*Among the most distinguished early houses in Prince George's County, Harmony Hall has been the home of many wealthy landholders over the centuries. A fine example of Georgian design with an I-house plan, it is also noteworthy for its spectacular location overlooking the Potomac River at Broad Creek. ⊗ Harmony Hall was constructed in the middle of the eighteenth century on a large tract of land known as Battersea. The brick plantation house was probably built for the family of Enoch Magruder. Its exceptional interior detail includes a graceful stairway,*

*paneled cupboard, and fretwork chair rails. After Magruder's death in 1786, his two plantations, Battersea and neighboring Want Water (page 34), passed to his daughter, Sarah Lyles. ⊗ This house was rented in 1793–94 by two brothers, John and Walter Dulaney Addison, and their brides, whose happy cohabitation inspired the new name, Harmony Hall. It remained in the Magruder-Lyles family until 1850. ⊗ Harmony Hall and Want Water were purchased in 1929 by Charles Collins, an early preservationist, and conveyed to the National Park Service in 1966.*

*Melwood Park, once the mansion house of a large tobacco plantation near Upper Marlboro, is a rare survivor of early county architecture, designed in a formal Georgian style. Of particular interest are its Flemish-bond brick exterior, covered with stucco scored to look like ashlar block; the sixteen-over-sixteen-light windows; and its interior paneling.* ✺ *It is believed that the original section (later replaced by the current kitchen wing) was built by William Digges, a prominent merchant and tobacco planter, about 1729. The property was inherited by his son, Ignatius, who probably built the main block about 1750. George Washington's diary gives numerous accounts of visits to Melwood Park.* ✺ *The house was raised to two stories about 1800, resulting in the uneven pitch of its roof. After 1825 it was acquired by John Pumphrey and later divided into smaller farmsteads. The Pumphreys removed the original section, replacing it after the Civil War with the present kitchen wing. Reduced to a farm of 38¼ acres from the original 1,050 acres, Melwood Park was tenanted by the Norfolk family from 1899 to 1988. Few changes have been made to the house, which is still without indoor plumbing and central heat.*

*Wyoming, the plantation home of the Marbury family, stands at the top of a ridge overlooking the Piscataway Creek Valley. The Marbury family first settled here in 1693 on land granted to Francis Marbury, an English immigrant. The politically prominent Marbury family had large land holdings in the Piscataway area throughout the eighteenth, nineteenth, and twentieth centuries.* ⊕ *Wyoming is a well-preserved example of a substantial, early settlement-period dwelling in the southern Tidewater tradition, distinguished by pent chimneys and telescoping additions. Evidence suggests that the main block of the house began as a smaller, three-bay dwelling with a basement kitchen; this was expanded in the last quarter of the eighteenth century with two more bays and the addition of fine, Federal-period interior trim. A separate kitchen building of heavy timber framing with brick nogging (see page 23) was con-nected to the main block by a two-story addition about 1850. South of the house is a small family cemetery located in a grove of locust trees looking toward the valley.* ⊕ *In addition to operating the tobacco plantation, Francis Marbury was appointed constable of the Piscataway Hundred and served as a justice of the county court. The plantation went to his son and later to his grandson Luke Marbury II, who is credited with the construction of the current house. Luke Marbury II served as a justice of the peace and county commissioner, and he represented Prince George's County at the first Constitutional Convention held in Annapolis in 1776.* ⊕ *Wyoming remained a tobacco plantation and the principal residence of the Marbury family for many generations, until it was purchased by the current owners in 1973. It is an outstanding and rare survivor of the county's early plantation houses.*

### ST. PAUL'S CHURCH

*Completed in 1735, St. Paul's Episcopal Church in
Baden is the oldest surviving church in the county
and reflects the establishment of the Church of
England in Maryland. St. Paul's Parish was one of
thirty parishes created in the Maryland colony in
1692. When Prince George's County was established
four years later, it included two of these parishes, one
of which was St. Paul's. ⊛ Although it has undergone
two substantial alterations, St. Paul's Church retains
a significant amount of its original structure. The
same construction specifications were soon adopted for
St. Thomas's Church in Croom (see page 44). Now
enlarged and cruciform in plan, St. Paul's 1794
entrance features a square lead sundial, purchased
from London in 1751 and inscribed "*SIC TRANSIT
GLORIA MUNDI*.*" *The county designated the
church for the official observance of mourning after
the death of George Washington in 1799.*

*Beyond the Gothic wrought-iron fence, atop a knoll shaded by large trees, stands St. Thomas's Church, an important county and community landmark in Croom. A brick path winds its way to the front entry of the church, which is surrounded by a cemetery with the burial places of many old county families.* ❖ *St. Thomas's was built in 1742–45 as a chapel of ease for the parish of St. Paul's Church in Baden (see pages 42–43). Although it was constructed on the same plan used for St. Paul's in 1735, later changes to both churches give them dissimilar appearances today. In 1859 St. Thomas's was renovated under the direction of New York City architect John W. Priest, an associate of Andrew Jackson Downing who was influential in spreading early Gothic Revival architecture. Priest's work included replacing the original windows in Gothic style and adding an apse. The bell tower was erected in 1888, in memory of St. Thomas's most celebrated rector, Thomas John Claggett, the first Episcopal bishop consecrated in America.* ❖ *The excellent condition of the church is the result of a 1954 restoration, which was based on the original 1745 building contract but retained Priest's romantic Gothic additions.*

## MARKET MASTER'S HOUSE

Adjoining what was once the marketplace and tobacco inspection warehouse in Bladensburg, this small, 1½-story stone structure is believed to have been the home of the manager of the market. Built about 1765, when Bladensburg was an active tobacco shipping port, it is the only surviving structure in Bladensburg that just fulfilled the town's minimum dwelling size requirement, 20 by 20 feet, including a chimney of brick or stone. ⊗ It was built by Christopher Lowndes, who constructed and resided at Bostwick (see pages 46–47); Lowndes was a successful merchant and served in several public offices. The house remained in the possession of the Lowndes family for 118 years and today is one of only four pre-Revolutionary structures in Bladensburg. ⊗ Unlike other vernacular masonry buildings of the period, the Market Master's House is built not of local stone, but rather of quartz or mica schist, the nearest source of which is northern Montgomery County and Baltimore. It is possible that the stone was ballast carried in the transport ships that frequented the port of Bladensburg; traditionally, such ballast stone once littered the shore of the Eastern Branch at this once-thriving colonial town.

## BOSTWICK

*Bostwick was one of the earliest and is now one of the few surviving historic structures in the once-active port of Bladensburg. Located high on terraced grounds with a complex of historic outbuildings, Bostwick was built in 1746 for Christopher Lowndes, a merchant and manufacturer. The Georgian house has postmedieval English elements: a high-pitched, flaring, gabled roof and ornamental T-shaped end chimneys. In fact, Lowndes's English heritage may have flavored the design of the house, named after his family home in Cheshire. ✿ Lowndes's daughter, Rebecca, and her husband, Benjamin Stoddert, later resided at Bostwick. Stoddert was secretary of the navy under President John Adams and then secretary of war. Bostwick was purchased by James H. Kyner, grandfather of the current owner, in 1904. Kyner made extensive changes inside and out, giving the Georgian design an updated Colonial Revival look.*

## ST. BARNABAS'S CHURCH

*One of only two early Georgian-style churches in the county, St. Barnabas's Church in Leeland is the third church on this site. It was built on the eve of the American Revolution, during the rectorship of Jonathan Boucher, a passionate Tory who alienated the revolutionary patriots in his congregation and sailed for England soon after the church was finished.*
✸ *A two-story brick structure with a hip-on-hip roof, its walls are laid in Flemish bond. On one of the bricks that frame the central first-story window on the east side is a hand-inscribed legend: "AD July 3, 1774," when the church was nearing completion.*
✸ *In 1855 a Victorian remodeling was undertaken, but in the early 1970s the church was restored to its original appearance including herringbone brick flooring. Today it houses several original furnishings from the earlier church on the site, including the 1721 painting* The Last Supper *by Gustavus Hesselius.*

Belleview, an excellent example of a small early plantation house, represents a once common but now rare dwelling type. Located near Friendly, this vernacular frame residence in the architectural tradition of the southern Tidewater region began as a modest hall-and-parlor-plan house about 1792. Belleview underwent a number of modifications around 1830, evolving into a more sophisticated dwelling with fine Greek Revival moldings and mantels. ✸ The property on which Belleview is located was acquired in 1760 by Enoch Magruder, a wealthy landholder (see Harmony Hall, pages 36–37, and Mount Lubentia, pages 68–71). After Magruder's death in 1786, the property was left to his daughter, Ann Lowe, and it was probably for her family that the house was built; the date 1792 is carved into one of the original chimney bricks. Belleview became the home of her son, Lloyd M. Lowe, who inherited the property in 1798. A generation later Lowe enlarged the house, doubling its depth with the addition of a rear stairhall and flanking parlors, raising the roof, and adding dormers. ✸ The current house has a 1½-story, side-gabled main block with a flounder addition, plus a one-story kitchen addition with a loft. Belleview also includes a rare and interesting collection of outbuildings, among them a log meat house, a large corn crib, and one of the oldest tobacco barns in the county. ✸ In 1856 the property was conveyed to Lowe's daughter, Leonora, and her husband, James M. Steed, who further enlarged the house to include the present kitchen wing. Belleview remained the Steed family home until the late 1960s, when it was abandoned for a modern house on the property.

## SNOW HILL

Snow Hill near Laurel is one of several fine brick houses of the prominent Snowden family. The original house, constructed for Samuel Snowden about 1764, burned and was rebuilt, possibly using the original walls, just before his death in 1801. ⊛ The fact that it was rebuilt may explain why it is in the earlier Tidewater style. But, unlike other examples of this house type, Snow Hill has a full Georgian plan of two rooms on each side of a center hall—resembling other nearby Snowden family plantations such as Oaklands and Montpelier (see pages 54–57). ⊛ Snow Hill has nearly identical east and west facades, with the true front facing the Patuxent River. A log meat house stands near the house on the river side. The property remained in the Snowden family until 1865. The house was restored in 1940 by the Warren family and has been purchased by the Maryland–National Capital Park and Planning Commission.

Designated as a National Historic Landmark, Montpelier is the grandest of the many Snowden family plantations built in the Laurel area. Wealthy Quakers, the Snowdens dominated the local economy from the late 1600s with their iron works and later textile mills. Major Thomas Snowden built Montpelier about 1783 on the family estate, which at one time totaled 27,000 acres. Among the guests entertained here were George and Martha Washington and Abigail Adams. ✿ The stately two-story, hipped-roof Georgian mansion, with flanking hyphens and wings, is elegantly balanced and classically inspired. Its interior detailing—cornices with agricultural motifs, a round-arch china cabinet, and elaborate mantels—is without equal in the county. A terraced front lawn with formal boxwood gardens includes a rare hexagonal summer house from 1796. ✿ Montpelier remained in the Snowden family until 1888. Its kitchen and servants wing date from about 1916. The last private owner-resident was Breckinridge Long, assistant secretary of state under Presidents Wilson and Franklin Roosevelt. Montpelier was conveyed to the Maryland–National Capital Park and Planning Commission in 1961 and is open to the public.

## HIS LORDSHIP'S KINDNESS

*His Lordship's Kindness near Rosaryville is located on land granted by Lord Baltimore in 1703. The house was built for Robert Darnall in 1784–87 and is one of the grandest of several plantation houses owned by the county's wealthy planters during the late 1700s. Only His Lordship's Kindness and Montpelier (see pages 56–59), however, incorporate the stately, five-part plan characteristic of Palladian-influenced, late Georgian design. ⊗ The interior is as formal and balanced as the exterior. The entrance leads into an elegant center hall and elaborate stairway, which consumes almost one-third of the floor space. The finely appointed parlor and dining room are sepa-*

*rated by hallways from the private rooms to the rear. The kitchen and the family's private Catholic chapel likewise were kept in the wings, apart from the social spaces. To the front of the house is the carriage entry with a circular drive; the rear looks out over a terraced boxwood garden. The former plantation also retains early dependencies including a privy, smoke house, wash house, slave hospital, and pigeon cote. ⊗ The Sewall and Daingerfield branches of the family inherited the estate, known then as Poplar Hill, and many are buried in the private cemetery. This National Historic Landmark, buffered by an operating horse farm, is managed by a private foundation.*

## COMPTON BASSETT

*Compton Bassett, just east of Upper Marlboro, reflects the prosperity of the tobacco plantation system on which the county's economy was founded. Home to the Hill and Sasscer families since it was built in the 1780s, this fine late Georgian mansion, the second on the site, gracefully exhibits the refined aesthetic of the style, with its symmetrical balance, hipped roof, and classically inspired pedimented pavilion, pilastered frontispiece, Palladian windows, and dentiled cornice. The brick exterior was stuccoed in 1822, according to family papers, by James Hoban, architect of the White House. ✹ Inside are fluted pilasters, dentils, and paneled reveals. Southeast of the house is a small brick chapel used by the Hill family for private Catholic services, a reminder of the period when public worship was forbidden. Near the mansion are a brick dairy and meat house.*

Charles Town was the original, late seventeenth-century seat of government of Prince George's County. Today Mount Calvert, near Croom, is the only historic building still standing on its site. An exceptional Federal-style brick plantation house, it is distinguished by prominent gable-end pent chimneys, particularly elegant interior trim, and its spectacular location overlooking the confluence of the Patuxent River and the Western Branch of the Potomac River. ❀ The main block of the house was built late in the eighteenth century by John Brown. An 1809 advertisement following Brown's death provides an early glimpse of Mount Calvert. It was described as having "the advantages of an excellent fishing landing. The land is well adapted to the production of tobacco, corn and all kinds of grain. . . . a quantity of good meadowland. . . . abounds with wood and timber. The improvements are a good brick Dwelling house, two stories high, nearly new, a good kitchen, several good Tobacco houses and Barns, with every other necessary building, all in good repair." ❀ The property was purchased in 1835 by John Brookes, an Upper Marlboro merchant, who rebuilt the old kitchen and connected it to the main block.

## MOUNT LUBENTIA

*Since Mount Lubentia in Largo was built in 1798 by Dennis Magruder, it has been home to five generations of the family—and is one of the county's best examples of Federal architecture, noted for its fine decorative detail.* ⊕ *The central entrance has a particularly elegant enframement, with fluted pilasters, a semicircular fanlight, and a keystone arch enclosed by a pediment with dentil molding. The irregular Georgian floor plan incorporates an asymmetrical four-room layout. The larger of the two front spaces is taken up by a particularly handsome formal stairhall, whose stair rises along an interior wall, curves to form a long landing, and turns again to the second story. Dividing the stairhall from the rear passage is a large elliptical arch with fluted pilasters, reflecting some of the elements of the principal entrance. The parlors have decorative Federal-style mantels; in no two rooms are the moldings exactly alike.* ⊕ *The hipped-roof house stands in a wooded grove on a parcel of land that includes all of the immediate outbuildings as well as the remnants of a formal garden.*

PLEASANT PROSPECT

Dr. Isaac Duckett—described as one of the wealthiest planters in the state—first received a parcel of land called "Sprigg's Request" from Thomas Sprigg in 1788, following his marriage to Sprigg's granddaughter, Margaret Bowie. To this, Duckett added surrounding parcels, eventually amassing a plantation of more than 800 acres, and built Pleasant Prospect in 1798. ⊛ Inside, the house now follows the Georgian plan, with a center hall flanked by two parlors on each side. The interior finish includes cornice moldings and refined motifs such as garlands, swags, and urns on doorways and mantels. ⊛ Pleasant Prospect later became the home of the Ducketts' only daughter, Eliza, when she married John Contee in 1813. The Contees continued to add lands to their plantation; the area around it came to be known as Woodmore. ⊛ Pleasant Prospect remained in the Contee family until it was sold in 1868 to Jonathan T. Walker. His renovations in the 1880s included construction of an imposing staircase in the center hall, replacing the smaller original alcove stair.

## RIVERSDALE

Riversdale, an outstanding combination of Federal-style Maryland architecture with European decorative detail, was begun in 1801 by Henri Joseph Stier, a Flemish banker and art connoisseur. It was finished in the next decade by his daughter, Rosalie Stier Calvert, who had married into Maryland's most illustrious family. ✦ After her father returned to Antwerp in 1803, Rosalie wrote to him regularly, informing him about the construction and embellishment of the house and giving fascinating insights into Washington society and politics. Henri Stier's paintings, the first major collection of Old World art in the United States, remained at Riversdale until 1816. ✦ The Calverts' son, Charles Benedict, brought the plantation to the peak of its prominence. He was an innovative agriculturalist, U.S. congressman, and founder of the Maryland Agricultural College. The mansion later became the centerpiece of the Victorian subdivision Riverdale Park. Riversdale was purchased by the Maryland–National Capital Park and Planning Commission in 1949 and is open to the public.

## ADDISON CHAPEL

*Addison Chapel in Seat Pleasant occupies what has
been the site of an Episcopal chapel since 1696,
when John Addison deeded an acre of land for it.
The present Flemish-bond brick structure, built about
1810, shows traces of the original building, as well as
later Victorian changes that raised its roof and gave
it Stick Style details in the gable ends. ⊗ Resembling a simple meetinghouse, Addison Chapel has
long been associated with prominent families of the
Bladensburg area, many of whom (such as the Lowndes
and Stoddert families of Bostwick) are buried in the
cemetery that surrounds the church. ⊗ In recent
years, changing population patterns in this developed
area have greatly decreased the size of the congregation. As a result, Addison Chapel was deconsecrated
in 1990, and in 1991 it was conveyed to the Prince
George's County Historical and Cultural Trust.*

## MARIETTA

Built in 1813–16 for U.S. Supreme Court Justice Gabriel Duvall, Marietta in Glenn Dale includes on its grounds the jurist's unique law office dependency; its single room has a fireplace and a tight dog's-leg stair to the small loft room above. ✸ Marietta is a Federal-style brick house in the traditional I-house form, with a perpendicular wing. Moderate in size and restrained in its decorative elements, the house features an entrance with a semicircular fanlight. Windows on this south facade have stone lintels with central keystones. Interior trim in the main block is typical of the late Federal period: mantels have fluted friezes and pilasters and in some cases applied oval shell motifs. ✸ Duvall's son died in 1831, making the justice, at the age of eighty, the guardian of his minor grandchildren. It was at this time that the wing was constructed, increasing the living space of the house. Gabriel Duvall died at Marietta in 1844, but the property remained in his family for two more generations. It was deeded to the Maryland– National Capital Park and Planning Commission in 1968. Today Marietta serves as a house museum and as headquarters and library for the Prince George's County Historical Society.

## BOWIEVILLE

Bowieville, near Leeland, is the most sophisticated late Federal-style plantation house in Prince George's County. Its outstanding decorative elements begin with the classical entrance, which is framed by two sets of engaged Doric columns and crowned by a semielliptical leaded fanlight; some of these elements are repeated in the formal parlors inside. The kitchen originally was located in the basement of the east wing, as a large cooking fireplace and built-in oven show. ❀ Constructed of brick and covered with stucco, Bowieville was built in 1819–20 by Mary Bowie on property inherited from her father, Maryland Governor Robert Bowie. She died only a few years later, and the property was sold in 1846 to William J. Berry, one of the county's wealthiest planters. Throughout the Berry family ownership, until the eve of World War II, Bowieville was a center of county society, the scene of many well-publicized balls, receptions, and other social events. Although Bowieville has been neglected in recent years, its decorative details are virtually intact and it is of exceptional architectural importance. Plans for its restoration are under way.

## PLEASANT HILLS

*Pleasant Hills is among the best examples of the
side-hall-and-double-parlor plan plantation houses
from the early 1800s. Located near Upper Marlboro,
it was built in two parts, with an 1830 main block
added to the original 1807 structure.* ✿ *The house
has fine Federal and Greek Revival interior details,
including faux ornamentation such as wood-grained
doors and painted escutcheons. Its plan incorporated
a "best parlor" for guests and a less formal back
parlor. A large hall passage served as the entry and
allowed for cross-ventilation, which was important
when such passages were used as living rooms in the
summer.* ✿ *Built by William B. and Zadock Sasscer,
the house stands atop a terraced knoll along with
outbuildings and tenant houses. The Sasscer and Hill
families who lived here, and still occupy the house,
were prominent in local politics and business.*

Weston was built early in the nineteenth century for Thomas Clagett VI, then one of the most prominent land owners in the Marlboro area. It stands on land that had been the Clagett family seat since the early 1700s. Weston has close associations with many other Clagett family properties, and the farmland around Upper Marlboro is dotted with dwellings that Thomas Clagett acquired or had built for the members of his large family. ⊛ Of these plantation homes, Weston is the earliest, the most substantial, and the only one built of brick. This handsome structure consists of a 2½-story main block and a 1½-story kitchen wing. The main block, originally only one room deep, is distinguished by fine detail in both the Federal and Greek Revival styles; the rear spaces were constructed a generation after the front. The kitchen wing probably incorporates an early free-standing structure, later joined to the main block by the connecting hyphen. ⊛ The house stands on a knoll among plantings of holly and boxwood at the end of a long tree-lined lane; nearby on a low hill is the family burial ground. This historic property has been home to nine generations of the Clagett family.

The congregation of Trinity Church in Upper Marlboro was formed in 1810 by Thomas John Claggett, Episcopal bishop of Maryland. By 1812 a frame church was built and dedicated. During the British invasion of August 1814, some of the church records were damaged when British troops passed through Upper Marlboro. ⊗ In 1845 the decision was made to build a new church, and a plan by Robert Cary Long, Jr., a prominent Baltimore architect, was chosen. Finished in December 1846, Trinity Episcopal Church is now a fine example of Gothic Revival architecture. Originally this brick structure had a simple front-gabled form; the present entry tower was added in 1896 to celebrate the fiftieth anniversary of the church. This tower has decorative brick bonding and corbelling and an ornamental crenellated parapet. The recently refurbished interior is lighted by Gothic-arch memorial stained-glass windows, and the gallery in the rear is dominated by a large pipe organ. ⊗ With its quiet cemetery setting and its early historical associations, Trinity Church is an important landmark in the town of Upper Marlboro, one long associated with the families of the surrounding area.

THE COTTAGE

Important elements in Prince George's County's agricultural economy and landscape, large farm complexes such as the Cottage were developed by prominent families during the nineteenth century. A three-part frame plantation house, with a telescope plan, the Cottage stands on rolling farmland west of Upper Marlboro. ✹ The main block was built in the 1840s for Charles Clagett, son of Thomas Clagett VI of Weston (see page 84). It is a good example of the era's popular side-hall-and-double-parlor plan. The central section dates from just before the Civil War and the small kitchen wing from approximately 1880. The cornices of all three sections are ornamented by deeply profiled jigsawn brackets. ✹ A short distance from the house are three domestic outbuildings, including a group of barns and a unique ice house whose oval brick substructure extends nearly eighteen feet into the ground. The largest of the barns incorporates a framing system and poles designed to allow tobacco to be hung to dry. This barn also houses an old tobacco press used to pack tobacco into hogsheads. The Cottage is now owned by the Chesapeake Bay Foundation and is devoted to environmental education.

## MELFORD

*A model of the side-hall-and-double-parlor plan
house, Melford near Bowie is one of only three known
examples of this plan built in brick; its two-story
semicircular bay, with its wide chimney stack and
pseudo-Palladian window, is unique.* ⊛ *Built in the
1840s by Dr. Richard Duckett, the house's interior
has rustic but bold Greek Revival decorative elements.
Also on the property are an attached brick and sandstone kitchen wing and two frame outbuildings: a
slave quarter that was converted into a farm office
and a small meat house with a pyramidal roof. To the
east are terraced gardens, falling away from the house
on three levels.* ⊛ *After the Civil War, Melford was
sold to local merchant Richard Hardisty, whose
family lived here until 1984. The property around
Melford is now undergoing development as the
Maryland Science and Technology Center.*

## COFFREN HOUSE AND STORE

*Small country stores were once a familiar part of the rural landscape of Prince George's County. John Coffren's store and post office in Croom, built about 1853, is a utilitarian structure, simple in design and void of ornamentation. Its interior remains virtually intact, providing a rare glimpse of a nineteenth-century rural community institution. ⊛ The interior consists of one large room with a counter running along each side and across the rear. The walls are lined with shelves for displaying merchandise, with large bins beneath, and a postal window is located near the front entry. In a county so shaped by agriculture, general merchandise stores provided essential items that families could not produce themselves on the farm, and they were also important social centers. ⊛ John Coffren's success allowed him by 1860 to build a handsome frame residence adjacent to the store. After his death in 1874, his widow continued to operate the store until 1893. The complex was then sold to Jeremiah Ryon, whose daughter and son-in-law managed the store until it was finally closed in 1948.*

The residence for a small plantation, Woodstock was built in the 1850s—the peak years of wealth and tobacco production in Prince George's County, just before the upheaval of the Civil War. After the war, this Upper Marlboro farm became a typical example of the Reconstruction era's breakup of plantations. Smaller farmsteads then became the norm in the county. ⊛ Woodstock's main block was built for Washington Custis Calvert, one of seven sons of Edward H. Calvert of Mount Airy. The younger Calvert married in 1851 and received 100 acres of his father's plantation, to which he added 220 more. Designed in the popular side-hall-and-double-parlor plan, the house is attached by a connecting hyphen to an older kitchen building. Less ornate than other examples of this traditional house form, Woodstock's Greek Revival detailing is elegantly understated; the applied ornament—in the painted detailing on the stairway, doors, and baseboards—is an interesting, noteworthy attempt to upgrade this somewhat modest dwelling. ⊛ In 1860 the farm was sold to James Beall Belt, a farmer and proprietor of a mercantile business, James B. Belt & Son, in nearby Upper Marlboro. The property remained in the family until 1973, when it was purchased and restored by the present owners.

## WARINGTON TOBACCO BARN

The Warington Tobacco Barn in Mitchellville is a strong reminder of the county's antebellum tobacco economy. ⊛ Built shortly before the Civil War by Marsham Waring, a successful planter, the barn has a braced frame and steeply pitched gabled roof. The siding is vertical board, some of which is handsplit, and the roof is covered with wood shingles. A low shed extends from each of the four elevations, giving the barn its distinctive profile. Based on evidence provided by nail holes in some places, and a lack in others, the long side sheds appear to be original, while the shorter end sheds are later additions. Hewn corner posts are pegged to the hewn top plate.

⊛ Although Waring's agricultural pursuits were diverse, his principal crop was tobacco. At the time of his death in 1860, his estate included 100,000 pounds of tobacco plus thirty-three hogsheads in Baltimore. Waring's daughters and granddaughter Amelia Belt inherited the property, which was sold in 1937 to Newton H. White, who developed it into a model dairy farm (see pages 132–33). White's widow sold the entire farm in 1971 to the Maryland–National Capital Park and Planning Commission. The barn is a prominent and picturesque landmark, the best surviving nineteenth-century tobacco barn in Prince George's County.

## HAZELWOOD

*Hazelwood stands on a bluff overlooking the Patuxent River near the site of the vanished port town of Queen Anne. ⊛ This unusual frame house encompasses three distinct periods, dating from the Revolution to the Civil War. The gambrel-roof home of Revolutionary War Major Thomas Lancaster Lansdale was enlarged in 1803 with the addition of a separate Federal-style structure. A three-story Italianate section was built about 1860, joining the two earlier parts. ⊛ Each section is distinguished by period detail. In the oldest a patent bake oven is built in next to the kitchen fireplace. The Federal section features an interior arch with fluted pilasters and a molded keystone. The central part has exterior latticework arches and a balustrade. ⊛ Included among the outbuildings is a brick combination meat house—privy, unique in the county. Hazelwood is now owned by the Maryland—National Capital Park and Planning Commission.*

## BOWLING HEIGHTS

*As the Civil War brought an end to the plantation system on which the county's economy had been based, large plantations were gradually broken up and smaller, more agriculturally diversified farms were created. John D. and Jemima Bowling were among this new breed of planter, and their home outside Upper Marlboro, Bowling Heights, was among the most elaborate farm residences built in this era.* ⊛ *Although the complex design from about 1870 suggests an architect or pattern-book plan, no evidence of either has been found. A richly orna-mented interpretation of the Victorian Gothic style, Bowling Heights has Stick Style and Eastlake motifs that were popular in urban areas but rarely found in rural Maryland. Nearly identical to Villa de Sales, built just a few years later for John Bowling's sister in Aquasco, it is the most fully expressed example of this style in Prince George's County.* ⊛ *An unusual feature of Bowling Heights is the attached chapel, a carry-over of the private chapels built by a number of wealthier residents before the Revolutionary War, when Catholics were denied public worship.*

## P. A. BOWEN HOUSE

*A visible landmark in the rural community of Aquasco, the Bowen House is an unusual Victorian frame farmhouse—notable for its outstanding Italianate decorative detail. It stands amidst a complex of nineteenth- and twentieth-century farm outbuildings.* ✿ *The house was built in 1870 by Philander A. Bowen, who at that time moved his family from Washington, D.C. Bowen was a teacher, successful planter, and member of the vestry of St. Paul's Church in Baden. His son served as the community physician, and the family remained influential in Aquasco for many years.* ✿ *The main block of the house features the side-hall-and-double-parlor floor plan that was popular in antebellum Prince George's County. The principal entrance is sheltered by a handsome wraparound porch with chamfered posts, ornate incised brackets, and pendants. The boxed cornice of the house is punctuated with jigsawn brackets, and the gabled dormers are highlighted with openwork vergeboards. Extending from the south gable end of the main block is a two-story wing, which has a bracketed boxed cornice similar to that of the main block; its low lean-to roof is masked by a unique parapeted false front, which gives added height and formality to the main facade—a unique feature among county houses.*

## SETON BELT BARN

*A product of the post—Civil War shift from tobacco to livestock and fodder crops, the Seton Belt Barn near Mitchellville is a rare decorative, vernacular agricultural building. It was built at the end of the nineteenth century to stable horses and store fodder on the Home Place farm, owned by Eleanor Lee Belt. ❁ An unusual jerkinhead roofline and profile are highlighted by decorated cupolas with jigsawn pendants. Remnants of dark red and robin's-egg blue paint on the window frames and cornice soffits indicate that the barn was highly ornamented. It has a central drive-through that divides the main level into a stable and corn crib—storage spaces. ❁ Seton Belt continued to manage the family farms until his death in 1959, after which the barn was adapted to hang tobacco. The entire second level is now devoted to tobacco and is accessible from the central passage by means of a neatly finished, partially enclosed staircase.*

Unusual for its location beyond a major urban center, the Ammendale Normal Institute (see pages 106–07) is an outstanding example of the eclectic architectural styles of the 1880s. Built in 1884–88, the brick landmark in Ammendale was established by the Christian Brothers as a school and novitiate. St. Joseph's Chapel, dating from 1880, stands on the grounds nearby. ✸ The institute, with its mansard roof and projecting wings, is more than 100 feet long. Behind the entry porch, a bell tower rises four stories; above its niche with a Madonna and child statue are an ironwork balustrade and an open bellcote with a steep pyramidal roof. The star motif (symbol of the Christian Brothers) appears in both the dormer windows and the iron grillework of the veranda. A gabled chapel wing extends to the rear. ✸ The small brick St. Joseph's Chapel boasts a large rose window and ornate jigsawn vergeboards adorning the eaves. The interior walls and ceiling are sheathed in pressed tin, with a pattern of fleurs-de-lys and palmettes and a rich multicourse cornice. ✸ The Christian Brothers added to their acreage and for many years ran a flourishing farm. The school and farm no longer operate, and the deteriorating institute building awaits rehabilitation.

## BALTIMORE AND OHIO RAILROAD STATION

*The Baltimore and Ohio Railroad Station in Laurel is the only surviving historic railroad station in Prince George's County.* ✿ *It was designed in 1884 by Baltimore architect E. Francis Baldwin in the picturesque Queen Anne style then popular. Baldwin designed at least thirty stations along the B&O in Maryland, including those in Hyattsville, Branchville, Riverdale, Berwyn, and Beltsville. The station displays typical Queen Anne detailing such as ornamental brickwork, an irregular hipped and cross-gabled roof, half-timbering, roof cresting, and decorative porch brackets.* ✿ *The B&O's Washington Branch, completed in 1835, was the first and most important of three rail lines through Prince George's. Its presence greatly affected Laurel's growth, providing transportation essential to development. Laurel was once the largest town in the county and the center for industry in an otherwise agricultural economy.*

*One of only a few county homes with outstanding Stick Style detail, the Holden House in Hyattsville was built in 1883 for Frederick Augustus Holden by local contractor George N. Walker. Holden served as a town commissioner after Hyattsville was incorporated in 1886.* ✦ *The frame house has a hipped and cross-gabled roof and a T-shaped floor plan. The south facade is dominated by a large cross gable in the upper stories; its deeply overhanging eaves are deco-rated with two long, unusual scissor trusses marked with a diamond pattern. The surface behind the trusswork is further embellished by a sawtooth border in the siding. In the rear parlor, a wood mantel on the corner fireplace features glazed tiles depicting scenes from Shakespearean plays.* ✦ *The Holden House remained in the family until 1926. On the adjoining lots to the east stands the house built in 1897 by Holden's brother, Louis (see page 114).*

## O'DEA HOUSE

This Queen Anne—style frame house was built in 1888 by the Charlton Heights Improvement Company in the newly platted subdivision of Charlton Heights, now known as Berwyn Heights. Like several other model houses erected there, it was built from a design by the Cooperative Building Plan Association, distributed by Robert W. Shoppell. ⊛ The main facade of the house features a three-story octagonal tower, framed by a porch with chamfered bracketed posts.

Beyond the plain board siding of the first story, the surfaces are varied by a number of ornamental coverings, including scalloped and fish-scale shingles. The shallow pyramidal roof of the tower is adorned with a metal acorn finial. A tall corbelled brick chimney is set at an angle behind the tower, serving a fireplace in the octagonal front parlor. ⊛ Highlighted by its three-story tower, the O'Dea House is one of the county's best Victorian pattern-book houses.

## HOLDEN-SWEETING HOUSE

*The Holden-Sweeting House is another fine example of a suburban dwelling with Queen Anne—style decorative detail. This handsome house stands in the town of Hyattsville and was built in 1897 by Louis Holden on lots that adjoin the residence built by his brother in 1883 (see page 112).* ✤ *Louis Holden built a very different style structure from that of his brother, however. It is a spacious frame house whose lines are varied by gables, dormers, projecting bays, and an oriel window. A variety of paneling enlivens the surfaces of the 2½-story house, including gables*

*ornamented with geometric paneling. An oriel window and a sleeping porch with a spindle frieze are other notable design features. The main entrance of the house leads into a formal stairhall, one of four key spaces. Pocket doors open from the stairhall into the front parlor, which has a Classical Revival mantel at a diagonally placed false fireplace. A spindle frieze forms a decorative grille between the stairhall and the kitchen. Both the Holden-Sweeting and Holden houses are noticeable landmarks in the Victorian residential area of Hyattsville.*

## WILLIAM W. EARLY HOUSE

William W. Early was general manager of the Southern Maryland Railroad, and this 1907 house in Brandywine, along the rail line, served as both his home and office. ⊛ One of the best examples of its type still standing in Prince George's County, the Early House is a notable frame dwelling in the Queen Anne style. Distinguished by a two-story octagonal corner tower and exuberant surface decoration, the house is large and roughly square. Cornices return, or continue, around all gable ends. Siding in the gables consists of alternating courses of fishscale and scal-

loped shingles; the vergeboards have jigsawn tracery and pendants. Across the main facade on the south side of the house is a one-story wraparound veranda with turned posts, jigsawn brackets, and a spindle frieze. ⊛ William W. Early was one of the grandsons of the merchant who owned much of the land that became Brandywine. His house is the most outstanding surviving dwelling of the Early family, which had great social and economic influence in the community. Today it is a prominent landmark in the old railroad village of Brandywine.

## ABRAHAM HALL

Rossville, where this benevolent society lodge for blacks was built in 1889, was first subdivided in 1886. The lots were purchased by a group of freedmen who worshiped at Queen's Chapel and farmed and worked at the Muirkirk Iron Furnace, both nearby. The largest lot was purchased by the Benevolent Sons and Daughters of Abraham, who constructed one of the first buildings, Abraham Hall, as a meetinghouse. Members were assured emergency financial assistance—a kind of insurance not otherwise available. ⊛ The hall is a two-story, front-gabled building with a small side kitchen wing. The interior consists of one large meeting room on each floor; on the first story, the room is extended to include a raised stage at the rear. ⊛ After the first Queen's Chapel was destroyed by fire, Abraham Hall served as the local Methodist meetinghouse and also as a schoolhouse. The most substantial building in Rossville, it is still the focal point of the community. One of two known surviving nineteenth-century black benevolent society halls (see also page 117), Abraham Hall was restored with public funds in 1991.

## ST. MARY'S BENEFICIAL SOCIETY HALL

*The second of two surviving benevolent society lodges, St. Mary's Hall was for a century the center of the social, religious, and charitable activities of the black Catholic community of Upper Marlboro. St. Mary's Beneficial Society was organized in 1880 to provide financial aid for emergencies as well as death benefits for its members, who paid a fee as well as small monthly dues.* ❀ *The one-story lodge building, which served the parishioners of St. Mary's Church, was completed in 1892. In form and plan, St. Mary's was similar to school buildings of the period—*

*smaller and more modest than Abraham Hall in Rossville (see page 116). During the 1898–99 construction of the present St. Mary's Church, the lodge was consecrated and used temporarily for services.* ❀ *After membership decreased, the St. Mary's Society sold the building to a group of attorneys, who have restored and converted it into a law office. With this modern adaptation, St. Mary's Beneficial Society Hall remains a landmark in Upper Marlboro and an important reminder of the social and cultural heritage of blacks in Prince George's County.*

## ST. IGNATIUS CHURCH

When it was consecrated in 1891 Cardinal James Gibbons of Baltimore called this Oxon Hill structure "the prettiest little church in southern Maryland." Today the church, which fronts directly on the old road between Upper Marlboro and the Alexandria ferry, remains the finest Queen Anne–style ecclesiastical landmark in Prince George's County. Contractor Charles Beers of Anacostia built it for $5,000. ❂ Contrasting textures such as board-and-batten siding, clapboard, and scalloped shingles are used to enliven the building's surfaces. The steep gabled roof, bell tower with steeple, buttresses, and high arched windows all emphasize its verticality. The interior is as exuberant as the exterior: the walls and ceiling are covered with wainscoting and beaded boards in alternating patterns, reflecting details of the exterior siding. The center aisle has a barrel-vaulted ceiling with ribs springing from fluted square posts. ❂ In the church's well-shaded cemetery, graves bear the names of some of the county's oldest Catholic residents, including the Hill and Brooke families. The first St. Ignatius Church was founded on this site in 1849 as a mission under the charge of the pastors of St. Mary's Catholic Church of Alexandria, Virginia.

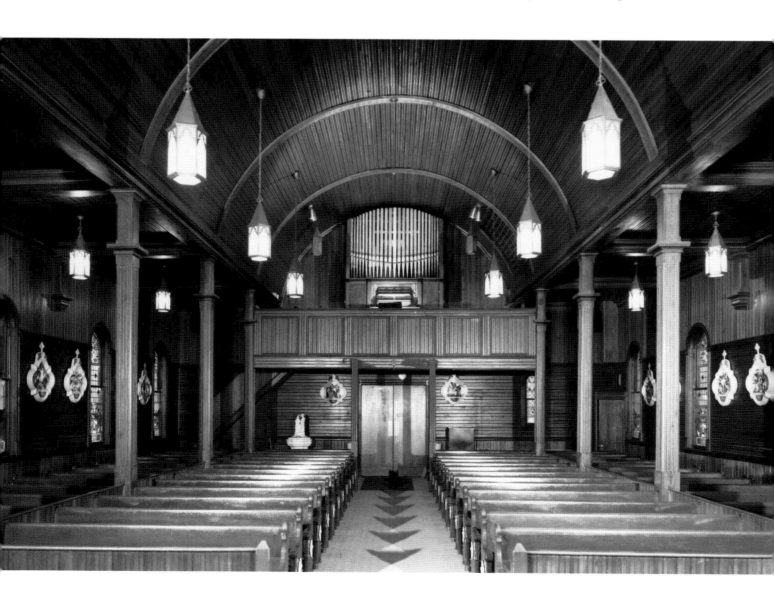

HOLY FAMILY CATHOLIC CHURCH

*Holy Family Church was built in 1890 to serve
the black Catholic community of the Woodmore-
Mitchellville area. Construction was undertaken by
the parishioners themselves, black and mulatto residents, most of whom made their living as tenant
farmers. The land was donated by Isaac and Willie
Ann Wood, members of the white-majority Sacred
Heart Church at White Marsh who recognized the
need for a local mission for blacks. ⊛ Holy Family
displays fine Gothic and Stick Style elements and
features a wood-paneled vaulted ceiling with exposed
roof trusses. The church became its own parish in
1938, under the Ministry of Black Churches, and
now receives its pastorship through the Diocese of
Washington. ⊛ With increased suburban development
of this area beginning in the 1960s, there has been
an influx of white families who have joined the
church. It is in excellent condition, having undergone
renovation and restoration work in 1983–84. Holy
Family Church is a local landmark and a site of considerable significance to the black Catholic community of Prince George's County.*

HYATTSVILLE HARDWARE STORE

*Hyattsville Hardware Store, prominently located along the main street of Hyattsville, is a rare, intact, late nineteenth-century commercial structure. It is one of only a few survivors from the town's early business district: most stores were replaced, beginning in the 1930s, with uniform commercial strips that now predominate. The building was originally used as a blacksmith shop and wagon and carriage manufactory. By 1911 it was a firehouse, and from 1913 to 1992 a hardware store. ⊛ Original interior features include a pressed-tin ceiling, built-in wood shelving,*

*and assorted display cases, cabinets, and bins. The shelf-lined walls harken back to the days of full-service shopping. ⊛ The building's painted sign along the cornice is an example of a now-vanished advertising tradition. This sign is all that remains of the handpainted advertising that once covered the entire west front and south side of the store, executed by Hasson and Haynes, house and sign painters of Hyattsville. Large painted signs of this type were made popular during the early age of the automobile, intended to catch the eye of the passing motorist.*

Both Belair Stables and Belair Mansion (see page 35) reflect a long history of thoroughbred horse breeding. Provincial Governor Samuel Ogle of Belair acquired Spark and Queen Mab, the two famous horses that began the Belair thoroughbred tradition. The estate's modern era of fame was launched with Belair's purchase by James T. Woodward at the end of the nineteenth century. ⊛ The stables building he added in 1907 is a dignified stone-and-brick structure consisting of a hipped-roof main block built of local sandstone with two brick shed rows. A central drive-through arch is the focal point of the building, which houses a carriage room, tack and feed rooms, and living quarters. Each shed row contains several wooden box stalls accessible by a long stepped corridor paved with brick. ⊛ Continuing the thoroughbred tradition started by Governor Ogle, Woodward, his nephew and heir, William Woodward, and his grand-nephew trained the noted horses Gallant Fox and Omaha, which won the Triple Crown of racing. Belair's Nashua was the Horse of the Year in 1955. ⊛ Following the estate's purchase by the Levitt Corporation, the city of Bowie acquired it and has opened the stables and the mansion for tours.

Governors Bridge crosses the Patuxent River near Bowie, joining Prince George's with Anne Arundel County. Erected in 1912, it is one of only two surviving truss spans in the county. ⊕ The bridge marks the site of a river crossing since colonial times, around which a small community formed during the late nineteenth century. Crossings were generally by ferry rather than by bridge, making this a unique site. The name "Governors Bridge" is derived from the use of this crossing by two eighteenth-century Maryland governors, Samuel Ogle and his son Benjamin, who lived at nearby Belair Mansion (see page 35). The crossing at this location would have been their standard route between Belair and the capital in Annapolis. ⊕ Governors Bridge is a steel, single-span Pratt through-truss bridge, composed of four panels measuring approximately 105½ feet long and 13 feet 7 inches wide. The Pratt truss was patented in 1844 by Thomas and Caleb Pratt and is distinguished by heavy vertical beams acting in compression and thin diagonal eyebars acting in tension. Many truss bridges were erected nationwide between 1850 and 1925. The manufacturer of Governors Bridge is unknown.

Locally known as the Castle, the Hyattsville Armory is notable for its medieval style as well as for serving as the home of Company F, the first American Legion Post in the county (1919). The armory was built by the state of Maryland in 1918 to house components of the First Maryland Infantry's Company F. It was the first armory in Prince George's County and the fifth in the state, and it may have served as a prototype for a number of other armories designed by state architect Robert Lawrence Harris. ❀ Built of irregularly coursed ashlar granite, the armory has a rounded central pavilion flanked by three-story squared crenellated towers. Some of its outstanding details are a central crenellated parapet with the seal of Maryland carved in limestone and stepped buttresses that mark the bays of the ell wing. ❀ Company F was formed in 1912 and was later joined with the Fifth Maryland Infantry Regiment to form the 115th Infantry, 29th Division. Veterans from the 29th Division were involved in the formation of the American Legion in 1919. Company F vacated the armory in 1972, and during the 1980s it was renovated for use as a restaurant and theater. Most recently it has been adapted for church services.

## GREENBELT CENTER ELEMENTARY SCHOOL

*This striking school opened in 1937 as the focal point for the nationally known planned community of Greenbelt. A Depression-era experiment in social and economic welfare, Greenbelt was constructed as one of three "green towns" by the Resettlement Administration, an outgrowth of Franklin D. Roosevelt's New Deal. The towns were developed to provide useful work to the unemployed, demonstrate the soundness of garden-city planning principles, and provide attractive housing for families of moderate means. ⊗ The design of the school evolved from the Art Deco and*

*Art Moderne styles popular during this period, emphasizing linear and geometric forms with a series of setbacks marked by streamlined buttresses, strips of casement windows with decorative low-relief panels, and a smooth wall finish relatively void of ornamentation. ⊗ The styling of the building focuses attention on a series of bas reliefs carved by Lenore Thomas, a Works Progress Administration (WPA) artist. The reliefs, which depict the precepts outlined in the preamble of the Constitution, reflect the social and economic concerns of the era.*

## NEWTON WHITE MANSION

*The Newton White Mansion in Mitchellville is an excellent example of an early twentieth-century estate house, one of the few in Prince George's County. Neoclassical in style, it was designed by noted architect William Lawrence Bottomley for Newton H. White, commanding officer of the U.S.S.* Enterprise. ⊛ *Built in 1939, the brick mansion has curved hipped roofs and porthole windows that suggest a naval theme. Framing the entry drive is a set of gateposts, each topped by a molded brick sculpture: a cock on one side and a hen with chicks on the other.* ⊛ *Commander White purchased the Warington farm in 1937, and the model dairy farm he developed there came to be known as the Enterprise Estate (see page 95). The 585-acre farm was sold by White's widow in 1971 to the Maryland–National Capital Park and Planning Commission. The mansion now serves as a reception hall, and the grounds are a golf course.*

HOWARD COUNTY

MONTGOMERY COUNTY

ANNE ARUNDEL COUNTY

DISTRICT OF COLUMBIA

Laurel

Ammendale

Rossville

Beltsville

Greenbelt

College Park

Berwyn Heights

Glenn Dale

Bowie

Riverdale

Hyattsville

Bladensburg

Woodmore

Mitchellville

Seat Pleasant

Largo

Queen Anne

Leeland

Prince George's County

Upper Marlboro ★

Oxon Hill

Rosaryville

Croom

Friendly

Broad Creek

POTOMAC RIVER

PATUXENT RIVER

Brandywine

Piscataway

Accokeek

Baden

CALVERT COUNTY

CHARLES COUNTY

Aquasco

N
W        E
S

0  1  2  3  4  5

in miles

# Designated Historic Sites of Prince George's County

*Abraham Hall.* Rossville. 1889. 🏛

*Accokeek Creek Archeological Site.* Accokeek. 3000 B.C.–17th century. U.S. Department of the Interior. NR, NHL

*Adams-Bowen House.* Aquasco. 1890

*Addison Chapel (St. Matthew's Church) and Cemetery.* Seat Pleasant. c. 1810, 1905. NR. 🏛

*Adelphi Mill and Storehouse.* Adelphi. 1796. M–NCPPC. 🏛

*Admirathoria.* Oxon Hill. late 18th century, altered 1870

*Ammendale Normal Institute and Cemetery.* Beltsville. 1884–88. NR. 🏛

*Ash Hill.* See *Hitching Post Hill*

*Ashland.* Upper Marlboro. 1867

*Ashland Hay Barn.* Upper Marlboro. 1830–50

*Baker-Holliday House.* Daniels Park. 1907

*B&O Railroad Station.* Laurel. 1884. NR. 🏛

*Baltimore-Washington Parkway.* Bladensburg to Laurel. 1954. NR

*William Barker House.* Aquasco. 1830, 1870

*Beall's Pleasure.* Landover. 1795. NR. 🏛

*Beechwood.* Leeland. 1913

*Belair Mansion and Cemetery.* Bowie. 1745, c. 1914. City of Bowie. NR. 🏛

*Belair Stables.* Bowie. 1907. City of Bowie. NR. 🏛

*Bellamy House.* Cheverly. 1925

*Bellefields and Cemetery.* Croom. 1720s. NR. 🏛

*Belleview and Cemetery.* Friendly. 1792, 1830. 🏛

*Bellevue.* Accokeek. 1840. NR

*Bells Methodist Church and Cemetery.* Camp Springs. 1910

*Seton Belt Barn.* Mitchellville. 1880. 🏛

*Belvidere.* Mitchellville. 1825, 1856

*Berwyn Heights School.* Berwyn Heights. 1922

*Billingsley.* Upper Marlboro. c. 1695, 1931. 🏛

*Black Walnut Thicket.* Baden. c. 1850

*Bleak Hill.* Upper Marlboro. 1852

*Bloomfield.* University Park. 1830, 1923

*Bostwick.* Bladensburg. 1746. NR. 🏛

*P. A. Bowen Farmstead.* Aquasco. 1870. 🏛

*Bowers-Sargent House.* Daniels Park. 1909

*Arthur G. Bowie House.* Glenn Dale. 1909

*Christ Church in Accokeek dates from 1748 and 1857.*

*Bowie Railroad Buildings.* Bowie. 1930s

*Bowieville.* Leeland. 1819–20. NR. 🏛

*Bowling Heights.* Upper Marlboro. c. 1870. NR. 🏛

*Boxlee.* Glenn Dale. 1923–24

*Boyden House.* Bowie. 1917

*Briarley Military Academy.* Beltsville. 1860s, 1911

*Brooke-Herring House.* Upper Marlboro. 1870, 1893

*Brookefield at Naylor.* Naylor. 1856, 1968

*Brookefield of the Berrys.* Naylor. 1810, 1840. NR

*Brookewood and Cemetery.* Croom. 1858

*Brookland M. E. Church.* See *Dorsey Chapel*

*Browning-Baines House.* Riverdale. 1896

*Brown's Tavern.* Beltsville. 1834

*Buena Vista.* Glenn Dale. 1850s

*Butler House.* Oxon Hill. c. 1850

*Calvert Mansion.* See *Riversdale*

*Carmody House.* Seat Pleasant. 1895, early 1900s

*Charles Hill.* Upper Marlboro. 1856

*Chelsea.* Oak Grove. 18th century, rebuilt c. 1825. M–NCPPC

*Cheltenham Methodist Church and Cemetery.* Cheltenham. 1879

*Chew's Bridge.* Upper Marlboro. 1898

*Christ Church and Cemetery.* Accokeek. 1748, 1857. 🏛

*Cissel House.* Berwyn Heights. 1888

*Coffren House.* Croom. 1860. NR. 🏛

*Coffren Store.* Croom. 1853. NR. 🏛

*College Park Airport.* College Park. 1909. M–NCPPC. NR

*College Park Woman's Club.* College Park. mid-19th century

*Compton Bassett, Dependencies, and Cemetery.* Upper Marlboro. 1780s. NR. 🏛

*Concord.* Capitol Heights. 1798. NR. 🏛

*Content.* Upper Marlboro. 1787, 1820s. NR. 🏛

*Cool Spring Farm.* Adelphi. 1790s, 1937

*Cory House.* College Park. 1890

*The Cottage.* Upper Marlboro. 1846, 1860. NR. 🏛

*Cottage at Warington.* Mitchellville. 1842. M–NCPPC

*Crandell-Cook House.* Lanham. mid-19th century, 1901

*Crandell-Rothstein House.* Upper Marlboro. 1840s

*Crawford's Adventure Spring.* Cheverly. Town of Cheverly

*Darnall's Chance and Tomb.* Upper Marlboro. c. 1700, renovated 1858, rebuilt 1988. M–NCPPC. NR. 🏛

*Digges-Sasscer House.* Upper Marlboro. 1845, 1880s. 🏛

*Dorsey Chapel (Brookland M. E. Church).* Glenn Dale. 1900

*Dueling Grounds.* Colmar Manor. M–NCPPC

*W. W. Duley House.* Croom. early 1800s, 1870s

*Augusta DuVal House.* Glenn Dale. 1894

*Duvall Bridge.* Laurel. 1907. U.S. Department of the Interior

*W. W. Early House.* Brandywine. 1907. NR. 🏛

*Eckenrode-Wyvill House.* Upper Marlboro. 1865

*Edelen House.* Piscataway. 1830s, 1926

*Ellerslie.* Upper Marlboro. 1895

*Elliott-Beall House.* Upper Marlboro vicinity. 1840s

*Fair Running.* Bowie. 1727, 1802. City of Bowie

*Fairview and Cemetery.* Collington. 1800. 🏛

*Fort Foote.* Oxon Hill. 1863. U.S. Department of the Interior. NR

*Fort Washington.* Fort Washington. 1814–24. U.S. Department of the Interior. NR. 🏛

*Dr. Charles Fox House.* Beltsville. 1886

*Fox's Barn.* Hyattsville. 1892

*Free Hope. See St. Paul's Baptist Church*

*Friendly School.* Friendly. 1890s, 1920s

*Furgang Farm.* Cheltenham. 1897

*Gallant House.* Adelphi. mid-19th century, 1920s

*Dr. Gibbons House.* Croom. 1893

*Kingston in Upper Marlboro was Victorianized in 1859.*

*D. S. S. Goodloe House.* Bowie. 1916. NR. 🏛

*Goodwood.* Upper Marlboro. 1800. 🏛

*Governors Bridge.* Bowie vicinity. 1912. State of Maryland. 🏛

*Greenbelt Center Elementary School.* Greenbelt. 1937. Prince George's County Board of Education. 🏛

*Green Hill.* Aquasco. 1830, 1941. 🏛

*Green Hill.* Hyattsville. 19th and early 20th centuries

*Grigsby Station Log Cabin.* Glenn Dale. c. 1840, moved and rebuilt 1983

*Grimes House.* Aquasco. 1800, 1850. 🏛

*Gross House.* Beltsville. 1916

*GSFC Magnetic Test Site.* Greenbelt. 1966. NASA. NR, NHL

*Gwynn Park.* T. B. 1857

*Hamilton House.* Mitchellville. 1870s. NR

*Hardy's Tavern.* Piscataway. 1790s. 🏛

*Harmony Hall.* Broad Creek. early to mid-18th century. U.S. Department of the Interior. NR. 🏛

*Hazelwood.* Queen Anne. late 18th century, 1803, 1860. M–NCPPC. 🏛

*Hilleary-Magruder House.* Bladensburg. mid-18th century. NR. 🏛

*His Lordship's Kindness (Poplar Hill) and Cemetery.* Rosaryville vicinity. 1784–87. NR, NHL. 🏛

*Hitching Post Hill (Ash Hill).* University Park. 1840. NR. 🏛

*Holbrook House.* College Park. 1927

*Holden House.* Hyattsville. 1883. 🏛

Holden-Sweeting House. Hyattsville. 1897. 🏛

Holy Family Church and Cemetery. Woodmore. 1890. 🏛

Holy Rosary Church and Cemetery. Rosaryville. 1928

Holy Trinity Church and Cemetery. Collington. 1836. 🏛

Holy Trinity Rectory. Collington. 1829, 1890s. 🏛

Horsehead Tavern. Horsehead. early 1800s, 1870s. 🏛

Dr. Hurtt House. Piscataway. 18th and early 19th centuries, 1912

Hyattsville Armory. Hyattsville. 1918. NR. 🏛

Hyattsville Post Office. Hyattsville. 1935. NR

Ingersoll-Muller House. Bowie. 1880s, 1897

Jarboe-Bowie House. Upper Marlboro. 1852

Kalaird. See Kalmia

Kalmia (Kalaird). Baden. 1840s, 1927

Kelly-Howerton House. Seabrook. 1880

Kildare. Oxon Hill. 1850, 1900

Kingston and Cemetery. Upper Marlboro. c. 1730, 1859. NR. 🏛

Kleiner-Dillon House. Berwyn Heights. 1888

Langley Park. See McCormick-Goodhart Mansion

Laurel High School. Laurel. 1899. Prince George's County. NR

LaValle House. Daniels Park. 1910

Locust Grove (Slingluff House). Woodmore. c. 1880

Mackall House and Cemetery. North Keys. 1790, 1910

McCormick-Goodhart Mansion (Langley Park). Langley Park. 1924

McDonnell House. College Park. 1896

McEwen House. Hyattsville. 1887. 🏛

McLeod-Forrester House. Beltsville. 1870s

Magruder Spring. Cheverly. Town of Cheverly

Magruder-Brannon House. Glenn Dale. 1912

Maple Shade. Glenn Dale. 18th century, 1860, 1890s

Marietta. Glenn Dale. 1813–16, 1830. M–NCPPC. 🏛

Market Master's House. Bladensburg. 1765. NR. 🏛

Marlboro Hunt Club. Upper Marlboro. 1855, 1880, 1920s

Mattaponi and Cemetery. Croom. 18th century, 1820. 🏛

Melford and Cemetery. Bowie. 1840s. NR. 🏛

Melwood Park. Upper Marlboro vicinity. 1750, early 1800s. NR. 🏛

Mitchellville Store Site and Storekeeper's House. Mitchellville. 1870s (store), 1906 (house)

Montpelier and Cemetery. Laurel. c. 1783. M–NCPPC. NR, NHL. 🏛

Montpelier of Moore's Plains. Upper Marlboro vicinity. mid-19th century, rebuilt 1940s

Mount Airy. Rosaryville. 1740, late 18th century. Maryland Department of Natural Resources. 🏛

Mount Calvert. Croom vicinity. 1790s. 🏛

Mount Clare. Melwood. 1859

Mount Hope. Cheverly. 1839, 1860s. NR

Mount Lubentia. Largo. 1798. NR. 🏛

Mount Nebo A. M. E. Church and Cemetery. Queen Anne. 1925

Mount Oak. Mitchellville. 1901

Mount Pleasant and Cemetery. Upper Marlboro vicinity. 1750. NR. 🏛

Mount Welby. Oxon Hill. c. 1800. U.S. Department of the Interior

Muirkirk Furnace Site. Muirkirk. 1847

B. D. Mullikin House Site. Mitchellville. 1870

Mullikin's Delight and Cemetery. Mitchellville. 1700s, 1800. 🏛

Northampton Site. Largo. 18th and 19th centuries. M–NCPPC

Nottingham Archeological Site. Nottingham. 500–1600. NR

Oakland. Upper Marlboro vicinity. 1820s, 1840s

Oaklands and Cemetery. Contee. 1790s. 🏛

O'Dea House. Berwyn Heights. 1888. NR. 🏛

Blanche Ogle House. Croom. c. 1890

Old Mill Place (Traband House). Upper Marlboro. 1894–97. NR

Orme-Shaw House. Beltsville. 1780, 1890

Overseer's House. Upper Marlboro. 1740s. 🏛

Oxon Hill Manor. Oxon Hill. 1929. M–NCPPC. NR. 🏛

Partnership and Cemetery. Mitchellville. 18th century, 1840s. 🏛

Pentland Hills. Upper Marlboro. 1830s

Perkins Chapel and Cemetery. Glenn Dale. 1861

Perrywood. Oak Grove. 1840, 1941

Pickett House. Berwyn Heights. 1890

Piscataway House. Broad Creek. late 18th century, rebuilt 1932

Piscataway Park Archeological Site. Accokeek. 3000 B.C.–18th century. National Park Service. NR

Piscataway Tavern. Piscataway. mid-18th century, 1810. 🏛

Plater House. Nottingham. 1901

Pleasant Hills. Upper Marlboro. 1807, 1830. NR. 🏛

Pleasant Prospect. Woodmore. 1798. NR. 🏛

Poplar Hill. See His Lordship's Kindness

Prospect Hill. Glenn Dale. early 19th century, 1940

Read-Low House. Riverdale. 1902

Ridgely Church and Cemetery. Largo vicinity. 1921

Riversdale (Calvert Mansion). Riverdale. 1801–07. M–NCPPC. NR. 🏛

River View Pavilion. Hatton Point. 1885, 1921

Rosemount. Baden. 18th century, 1835

*Rossborough Inn.* College
Park. 1803, 1938.
State of Maryland.
🏛

*Ryon House.* Bowie.
1903.
*Sacred Heart Church and
Cemetery.* Bowie.
1741, 1855, 1876. 🏛
*St. Barnabas's Church and
Cemetery.* Leeland.
1774. 🏛
*St. Barnabas Church and
Cemetery.* Oxon Hill.
1851. 🏛
*St. George's Chapel and
Cemetery.* Glenn Dale.
1892
*St. Ignatius Church and
Cemetery.* Oxon Hill.
1891. NR. 🏛
*St. James Hill.* Piscat-
away. 1830s. 🏛
*St. John's Church and
Cemetery.* Broad
Creek. 1766.
NR. 🏛
*St. John's Episcopal Church
and Cemetery.*
Beltsville. 1877
*St. Joseph's Chapel.*
Beltsville. 1880.
NR. 🏛
*St. Margaret's Church.*
Seat Pleasant. 1908
*St. Mary's Beneficial
Society Hall.* Upper
Marlboro. 1892. 🏛
*St. Mary's Church and
Cemetery.* Piscataway.
1904
*St. Mary of the Assumption
Church.* Upper
Marlboro. 1899
*St. Mary's Rectory.* Aquas-
co. 1848, 1856. NR
*St. Matthew's Church.* See
*Addison Chapel*
*St. Paul's Church and
Cemetery.* Baden.
1735. NR. 🏛
*St. Paul's (Free Hope)
Baptist Church.*
Bladensburg. 1818,
1908

*St. Thomas's Church and
Cemetery.* Croom.
1742–45. 🏛
*St. Thomas Methodist
Church and Cemetery.*
Horsehead. 1911
*Salubria.* Oxon Hill.
1830. 🏛
*Sasscer's Green.* Upper
Marlboro. 1820. 🏛
*Seabrook School.*
Seabrook. 1896.
M–NCPPC
*Seifert House.* Seabrook.
1880
*Sellman House.* Beltsville.
1905. U.S. Depart-
ment of Agriculture
*Shepherd-Sibley House.*
Hyattsville. 1906
*Silesia School.* Silesia.
1902
*Slingluff House.* See
*Locust Grove*
*Albert Smith House.*
Bowie. 1910
*Benjamin Smith House.*
Hyattsville. 1880s
*Harry Smith House.*
Riverdale. 1890
*Thomas W. Smith Farm
House.* Mount
Rainier. 1900
*Snowden Hall.* Laurel
vicinity. early 19th
century, 1939. U.S.
Department of the
Interior. 🏛
*Snow Hill.* Laurel.
1800. M–NCPPC 🏛
*Solitude.* Upper
Marlboro vicinity.
1840
*Souder House.* Temple
Hills. 1901
*Sportland.* Berwyn
Heights. late 18th
century, 1850
*Straining House.* Bowie.
1870
*Strawberry Hill.* Upper
Marlboro. 1869
*Sunnyside.* Aquasco.
1844. NR

*Mary Surratt House.*
Clinton. 1852.
M–NCPPC. NR. 🏛
*Talbott House.* Upper
Marlboro. 1840s
*Taliaferro House.* College
Park. 1893–97
*Taylor-Lofgren House.*
Berwyn Heights.
1909
*Terrett House.* Friendly
vicinity. 1910
*Traband House.* See *Old
Mill Place*
*Trelawn.* Upper
Marlboro. 1850s
*Trinity Episcopal Church
and Cemetery.*
Upper Marlboro.
1846, 1896. 🏛
*H. B. B. Trueman House.*
Aquasco. 1850
*Trueman Point.* Eagle
Harbor. 1860–1930
*Trumps Hill.* Upper
Marlboro vicinity.
1854
*Turner House and
Erickson-Roundell
Tomb.* Nottingham.
late 18th century
*J. E. Turner House.*
Aquasco. 1857
*Joshua Turner House.*
Rosaryville. 1880s
*Thomas J. Turner House.*
Upper Marlboro.
1850–55
*Union Methodist Church.*
Upper Marlboro.
1916
*Van Horn House.* Glenn
Dale. 1893
*Van Horn-Mitchell House.*
Deanwood. 1803
*Villa de Sales.* Aquasco.
1877. NR
*Walnut Grange.* Belts-
ville. 1805. U.S.
Department of
Agriculture
*Want Water Ruins.* Broad
Creek. c. 1710. U.S.
Department of the
Interior. NR. 🏛

*Waring's Grove.* Landover.
18th century, rebuilt
19th century
*Warington Tobacco Barn.*
Mitchellville. 1850.
M–NCPPC. 🏛
*Warren House.* Riverdale.
1913
*George Washington House.*
Bladensburg. 1760.
NR. 🏛
*Waverly.* Croom. 1855.
NR
*Webb-Brown House.*
Landover. 1870
*Welsh House.* Hyattsville.
c. 1890
*West End Farm.* Croom.
1855
*Weston and Cemetery.*
Upper Marlboro.
early 1800s. 🏛
*Wetherald House.* Berwyn
Heights. 1891
*Newton White Farm and
Cemetery.* Mitchell-
ville. 1939.
M–NCPPC. 🏛
*Williams Plains.* Bowie.
1813, 1840s. NR
*Wilson-Rawlings Farm-
stead.* Milltown. 1895
*Wolfe House.* Berwyn
Heights. 1889
*Wood House.* Aquasco.
early 1800s
*Woodlawn.* Oak Grove.
1858, renovated
1936
*Woodstock.* Upper
Marlboro vicinity.
1850s. NR. 🏛
*Woodyard Site.* Rosary-
ville vicinity. late
17th to mid-19th
century. NR
*Wyoming and Cemetery.*
Piscataway vicinity.
1760, 1800, 1850.
NR. 🏛
*Wyvill House.* Upper
Marlboro. 1889
*Ziegler Cottage.* Mount
Rainier. 1932

# Guide to Architectural Plans and Styles

THIS GUIDE SHOWS FIVE FLOOR PLANS AND ARCHITECTURAL STYLES COMMON IN PRINCE GEORGE'S COUNTY HOUSES. SOME PLANS SPAN MORE THAN ONE STYLISTIC PERIOD.

### Hall-and-Parlor Plan
Two rooms wide and one room deep; no stairhall or passage; 1½ stories; boxed-winder stair to a loft. The hall was for everyday use, the parlor for guests.

### Tidewater (1700–1800)
Early settlement type from the Chesapeake or Tidewater region; gabled or gambrel roof, 1½ stories; often a full-width shed-roof porch and paneled interiors.

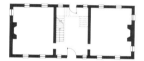

### I-House Plan
A center hall flanked by one parlor on each side; one room deep; two or 2½ stories. Many I-houses were enlarged with extensions to the rear.

### Georgian (c. 1710–1800)
Classically inspired; symmetrical in plan and facade; gabled or hipped roof; central entrance; dentiled cornice and full entablature; generally a center stairhall.

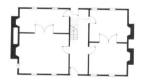

### Georgian Plan
A central stairhall flanked by rooms on each side; two rooms deep; two or 2½ stories. In an irregular plan, the stairhall may be to one side.

### Federal (1780–1830)
Similar to Georgian style above; entrance generally has a semi-elliptical leaded fanlight; entrance sometimes is placed to the side.

### Side-Hall-and-Double-Parlor Plan
A large entry and stairhall running the length of the structure; two adjoining parlors to one side; two or 2½ stories.

### Greek Revival (1820–60)
Adaptation of classical Grecian style, often with classical-order columns, frieze, and pediment; entrance has transom and sidelights.

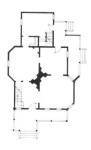

### Asymmetrical Plan
An asymmetrical arrangement created by towers, turrets, extended bays, and porches; side or center hall; side or rear wing; usually 2½ stories.

### Queen Anne (1880–1910)
Most ornamental of the Victorian styles, with Stick Style and Gothic details; ornamental surface coverings; exuberant jigsawn gable and porch details.

# Further Reading

Presented here are general publications that provide basic background information on the history of Prince George's County. These books can be found in the Prince George's County Memorial Library System, along with many others on more specific aspects of the county's history, including histories of particular communities, organizations, religious institutions, and families.

Bowie, Effie Gwynn. *Across the Years in Prince George's County*. 1947. 904 pages. Reprint. Baltimore: Genealogical Publishing Company, 1975.
Biographies and genealogies of the county's oldest families.

Floyd, Bianca P. *Records and Recollections: Early Black History in Prince George's County, Maryland*. Upper Marlboro: Maryland–National Capital Park and Planning Commission, 1989. 128 pages.
An overview of the history of African Americans in Prince George's County, with highlights of important individuals and communities.

Hienton, Louise Joyner. *Prince George's Heritage*. Baltimore: Maryland Historical Society, 1972. 223 pages.
A readable history of the county from its founding to 1800. Includes a map of tracts laid out before 1696.

Hopkins, G. M. *Atlas of Prince George's County, Maryland, 1878*. Frank F. White, Jr., ed. Riverdale: Prince George's County Historical Society, 1975. 48 pages.
A reprint of an 1878 county atlas showing property owners, with an index.

Prince George's County Planning Department. *Illustrated Inventory of Historic Sites*. Upper Marlboro: Maryland–National Capital Park and Planning Commission, 1990.
A photographic inventory, with a history and descriptions of more than 200 designated sites in Prince George's County.

Van Horn, R. Lee. *Out of the Past: Prince Georgeans and Their Land*. Riverdale: Prince George's County Historical Society, 1976. 422 pages.
A chronological account of events in the county's history through 1861, taken mainly from legal and government records and newspaper reports. Includes S. J. Martenet's 1861 map of the county and a bibliography of books and articles on county history.

Virta, Alan. *Prince George's County: A Pictorial History*. Norfolk, Virginia: Donning Company, 1991. 308 pages.
An excellent collection of rare historic photographs and other illustrations of county history, tied together with a highly readable history of Prince George's County from the colonial period to 1990.

# The Photography

JACK E. BOUCHER

"We did things the old-fashioned way" describes the photographic techniques used to record the landmarks of Prince George's County. A huge camera, by today's standards, with the once-familiar black cloth over the photographer's head, and metal cases of equipment all were required to record these structures to the exacting standards of the Historic American Buildings Survey.

Our Linhof Master TL view camera, only five years old, resembles the cameras of a century ago. It produces a 5-by-7-inch image, a size that is essential to architectural documentation because the image is large enough to permit study of tiny areas and minute structural details.

The Linhof camera also has numerous features not available on smaller cameras, such as swings, tilts, shifts, a rising and falling front and rear standard, adjustments needed to obtain razor-sharp focus and correction of perspective distortion—the tendency of lines to converge and buildings to appear to lean in photographs.

An average of six to eight exterior and two to five interior photographs were taken for each site. Included were a front elevation, a square-on view of the principal facade, and perspective and detail photographs. Interiors often showed entire rooms, staircases, attic truss systems, heating systems, and, in the case of St. Barnabas's Church, extreme close-ups of 200-year-old graffiti on bricks.

Seven large-format lenses were used, ranging in focal length from 90mm to 508mm, each with a variety of filters, including K-2, G, red 25, and polarizing, 180mm being the normal focal length for a 5-by-7-inch image. All camera adjustments, including composition and focusing, were done under 3x magnification on the camera ground-glass screen.

Lighting techniques varied according to the subject and circumstances. Natural light was enhanced when necessary by the use of 1,000- and 600-watt quartz lights, small-wattage spot lamps, 150- to 1,200-watt second electronic flash, and flashbulbs the size of 300-watt household bulbs. Many images, especially in structures lacking electricity, were captured by painting with light, a technique using many overlapping flashes to light, highlight, and backlight the subject.

Kodak TMAX black-and-white film was used and archivally processed to provide an anticipated 500-year life. Ten percent of the subjects also were taken in large-format color, using Ektachrome daylight or tungsten film as required; these transparencies, lacking archival stability, do not form a part of the HABS permanent record and are usable only as long as they last—a few years.

In many cases the HABS recording team—historian Catherine Lavoie and I—found structures so complex as to require more than a single day to document. Most images required half an hour to half a day each. This photodocumentation project, encompassing 900 photographs of sixty-two structures, is now preserved for posterity in the Library of Congress, providing a priceless record of one of Maryland's premier historic counties.

# Acknowledgments

This book is the result of a cooperative photodocumentation project between the Historic American Buildings Survey of the National Park Service and the Prince George's County Planning Department of the Maryland–National Capital Park and Planning Commission. Robert J. Kapsch, chief of HABS / HAER, and Gail C. Rothrock, preservation coordinator for Prince George's County, arranged the project sponsorship and funding. Initial selection of properties was made with suggestions from the Prince George's County Historic Preservation Commission, Prince George's Heritage, and the Prince George's County Historical and Cultural Trust. Catherine C. Lavoie, HABS historian, and Susan G. Pearl, M–NCPPC historian, assisted HABS photographer Jack E. Boucher in field work.

A grant from Prince George's Heritage helped develop the book concept, with initial support from Dale Manty, chairman. The book concept was developed by Diane Maddex of Archetype Press. Public support came from the Historic American Buildings Survey, a Certified Local Government grant through the Maryland Historical Trust, and the Prince George's County Planning Board. Within the Maryland Historical Trust, Michael K. Day, chief, Planning and Educational Outreach, and Orlando Ridout V, chief, Research, Survey, and Registration, provided valued advice.

At M–NCPPC a note of special appreciation is due Fern V. Piret, planning director, who endorsed the project and secured the support of the Prince George's County Planning Board. Thanks go also to A. R. Tankersley, chief, Area Planning Division, and Historic Preservation Section staff members Sandra Cross, administrative aide; Gary Thomas, planning technician; and Marina King and Howard Berger, architectural historians. Michael Petrenko, deputy planning director, and William F. Henaghan, budget coordinator for the Planning Department, as well as D. F. Bartholomew, Jr., in the Department of Finance, assisted with contracts.

Within HABS Paul Dolinsky, HABS chief, gave his support; and Alison K. Hoagland, senior historian, served as reader and adviser. Shelley Homeyer, architectural technician, executed the floor plans in the Plans and Styles guide.

The authors appreciate the review comments of Historic Preservation Commissioners Robert A. Crawley, Jane Eagen, Steven B. Rogers, and former Commissioners Alan Virta and Raymond W. Bellamy, Jr., as well as those of Frederick S. DeMarr and John M. Walton, Jr. Thanks go also to Margaret Yewell, Joyce Rumburg, Dick Charlton, and Patricia Williams.

Finally, the authors wish to thank the individuals who love and maintain the properties pictured in this book and who cooperated with the photography and other needs of the project: Frances Bowie, Frank Calhoun, H. C. B. Clagett, Jr., Guy Clark, Mr. and Mrs. Eugene Couser, Mr. and Mrs. Gerard Dunphy, Lynda and Daniel Filippelli, Mr. and Mrs. Raymond Garthoff, Carlton Huhn, Mr. and Mrs. John M. Myers, Mr. and Mrs. L. G. Sasscer, Jr., Dr. and Mrs. Robert Sasscer, Mr. and Mrs. Stephen Sonnett, Mr. and Mrs. Lester Sweeting, John M. Walton, and Mr. and Mrs. Tim Yatman.

# Index